Vegetarian Indian Cuisine

Savitaben J Koria

Matador
5 Weir Road
Kibworth
Leicester LE8 0LQ, UK
Tel: (+44) 116 2792299

Email: books@troubador.co.uk
Web: www.troubador.co.uk/matador

British Library Cataloguing in Publication Data.
A catalogue record for this book is available from the British Library.

ISBN 978 1 84876 391 3

Matador is an imprint of Troubador Publishing Ltd

Cover Design, Layout and Photos by:

Kuk Designs
Tel: 07801450 209
Email: sanjay@kukdesigns.com
website: www.kukdesigns.com

Photographs Copyright © Kuk Designs

Introduction

It is my great pleasure to introduce this cookery book to those who are vegetarian and who enjoy and love cooking for the family. I have tried to avoid using technical jargon in this book to make it easy for anyone to cook the most delightful dishes. This book is for those people who are proud of their cooking.

Follow the instructions and the recipes carefully and the resulting dishes will be both tasty and colourful. Welcoming guests with tasty food is a pleasant occasion for the family. Your friends and family will compliment you for being a super cook and hostess.

More and more people are choosing to be vegetarians and are looking for variety and tasty dishes. We are also getting more health conscious with our food today. This book has been written with such trends in mind. The use of oil and sugar is limited to reduce both calories, cholesterol and weight.

This book would not have been possible without the support and understanding from my husband, Jayanti, my son Pankaj, daughter-in-law Rakhi and my two daughters, Renu and Anju. They have all provided such encouragement to me in completing this book.

I wish you enjoy cooking and may you win many hearts with these delicious dishes!

Contents

Savoury Dishes

Sweet Dishes

Contents...

Useful information

These charts and guidelines are here to help you in the kitchen with measurements, information on ingredients and tips on equipment. It also provides a guide to the symbols that accompany each recipe in the book. All the recipes have been tested on a gas ring hob and an electric oven (for a fan oven, reduce the temperature by at least 10 degrees). If in doubt about how accurate your oven is, it may be wise to invest in an oven thermometer.

Measurements for bowl and cup sizes
Bowl – This should be approximately **12 cm in diameter (8 ounces)**
Cup – This should be approximately **8 cm in diameter (6 ounces)**

Linear measures

3mm	(⅛in)	2.5cm	(1in)	10cm	(4in)	20cm	(8in)
5mm	(¼in)	5cm	(2in)	12cm	(5in)	23cm	(9in)
1cm	(½in)	6cm	(2½in)	15cm	(6in)	25cm	(10in)
2cm	(¾in)	7.5cm	(3in)	18cm	(7in)	28cm	(11in)
						77cm	(30in)

30cm	(12in)
46cm	(18in)
50cm	(20in)
61cm	(24in)

Weights

10g	(¼ oz)	85g	(3oz)	250g	(9 oz)	750g	(1lb 10 oz)
15g	(½ oz)	100g	(3½ oz)	300g	(10 oz)	800g	(1¾ lb)
20g	(¾ oz)	115g	(4oz)	350g	(12 oz)	900g	(2lb)
25g	(scant 1oz)	125g	(4½ oz)	400g	(14 oz)	1kg	(2¼ lb)
30g	(1oz)	140g	(5oz)	450g	(1lb)	1.1kg	(2½ lb)
45g	(1½ oz)	150g	(5½ oz)	500g	(1lb 2oz)	1.25kg	(2¾ lb)
50g	(1¾ oz)	175g	(6oz)	550g	(1¼lb)	1.35kg	(3lb)
60g	(2 oz)	200g	(7oz)	600g	(1lb 5oz)	1.5kg	(3lb 3oz)
75g	(2½ oz)	225g	(8oz)	675g	(1½lb)	1.8kg	(4lb)

2kg	(4½lb)
2.25kg	(5lb)
2.5kg	(5½lb)
2.7kg	(6lb)
3kg	(6½lb)

Volume measures

1 tsp		75ml	(2½fl oz)	240ml	(8fl oz)	500ml
2 tsp		90ml	(3fl oz)	250ml	(9fl oz)	600ml
1tbsp (equivalent to		100ml	(3½fl oz)	300ml	(10fl oz)	750ml
3 tsp)		120ml	(4fl oz)	350ml	(12fl oz)	900ml
2 tbsp		150ml	(5fl oz)	400ml	(14fl oz)	1 litre
3 tbsp		200ml	(7fl oz)	450ml	(15fl oz)	1.2 litres
4 tbsp or 60ml (2fl oz)						

500ml	(16fl oz)	1.4 litres	(2½ pints)
600ml	(1 pint)	1.5 litres	(2¾ pints)
750ml	(1¼ pints)	1.7 litres	(3 pints)
900ml	(1½ pints)	2 litres	(3½ pints)
1 litre	(1¾ pints)	3 litres	(5¼ pints)
1.2 litres	(2 pints)		

Oven temperature

130 °C (250 °F/Gas ½)	190 °C (375 F/Gas 5)	Gas ¼ - ½ - very cool oven
140 °C (275 °F/Gas 1)	200 °C (400 F/Gas 6)	Gas 3 - low oven
150 °C (300 °F/Gas 2)	220 °C (425 F/Gas 7)	Gas 1-2 - very low oven
160 °C (325 °F/Gas 3)	230 °C (450 F/Gas 8)	Gas 4-5 - moderate oven
180 °C (350 °F/Gas 4)	240 °C (475 F/Gas 9)	Gas 6-7 - hot oven
		Gas 8-9 - very hot oven

Herbs & Spices

Spices play a very important role in cooking. They bring out the original flavour and make the food aromatic, attractive appetizing and most important easily digestible. Most spices have some medicinal value. Spices should be stored in airtight containers in a cool dry and dark place. Freshly ground spices release a lovely aroma.

They lose their flavour on being kept for a long time so it is advisable to buy whole spices and grind them as required. If you have to buy spices in powder form then do so in small quantities making sure that they are fresh at the time of purchase. Almonds, cashews and pistachios are used in many sweet as well as savoury dishes. They make the dishes tasty but rich in calories.

Given below are the essential and common condiments and nuts. The Hindi names are given in brackets.

Almonds (Badam)
Among nuts, almonds are most extensively used in cooking. They taste good in sweets, ice creams, confectionery, Indian sweets and desserts. Almonds combine successfully with savoury dishes vegetable preparations, soups, as well as salads. They are used whole blanched flaked slivered or toasted.

Anise (Suwa)
This is a light brown legume with a delicious nutty flavour. It is sprouted and used in making salads and sandwich fillings.

Aniseed (Saunf)
A small sweet smelling light green and oval shaped seed. In Western countries it is used to flavour wines and confectionery. In India aniseed is roasted and eaten after meals as a mouth freshener and to stimulate digestion.

Asafoetida (Hing)
It is available in lumps as well as in a grainy powdered form. It is a common practice to place one or two lumps into bottles containing powdered spices like chillies, cumin seeds, coriander seeds or turmeric powder in order to preserve them for the whole year. Powdered asafoetida is used in very small quantities (just a pinch) for flavouring many vegetarian dishes.

Bay leaves (Tej Patta)
These dry, light green, long and aromatic leaves are preserved in airtight bottles. Mostly used for flavouring pullaos and some curries, the leaves are left whole and are not actually eaten.

Black peppercorns (Kala mirch)
Fresh green peppercorns, in bunches are used in pickles. But the sun dried, hard, black, brittle seeds are commonly used in many Western and

Indian recipes. They are used whole or freshly ground.

Cardamoms (Elaichi)
An aromatic spice, generally sold in pods. There are 2 types one is dark brown and big (Badi Elaichi) with seeds inside and has a strong flavour. It is used whole for flavouring pullaos. The other is small with a light green pod and has black seeds and a pleasant smell. A cream coloured, plumper variety is also available, but it has less aroma. Cardamoms are extensively to flavour sweet dishes and also in many vegetable and rice dishes. Sometimes, cardamoms are used whole or the black seeds are powdered before use in a recipe.

Carom seeds (Ajwain)
Tiny brown seeds with a strong smell. They are generally used while preparing many Indian vegetables and pulses.

Cashew nuts (Kaju)
One of the favourite nuts used in the preparation of many Western and Indian dishes. Its subtle flavour and taste blends very well in many sweets as well as savoury dishes. It is a white, semi-circular nut with a thin brown shell, which comes off readily on roasting. One can buy shelled cashew nuts also. Roasted, salted cashew nuts are excellent as a cocktail snack.

Chillies (Hari mirch and lal mirch)
Generally, 2 types of chillies are used in cooking-fresh green ones (hari mirch) and dry red ones (lal mirch). Both varieties are quite pungent. If you want just the flavour without its pungency, then make a slit on the side of the chilli and shake out the white seeds from inside. Green chillies are used whole or cut into pieces or ground to a paste

before using. Red chillies are either used whole or ground to a paste.

Cinnamon (Dalchini)
This dried aromatic brown bark of the cinnamon tree. It is used in stick or powder form for sweets, cakes and curries. Sticks used for flavouring pullaos are removed at the time of eating.

Cloves (Laung or Lavang)
The dried aromatic flower buds of the clove tree. Cloves are used whole or in powdered form in many sweets, savouries and spice powders. Clove oil possesses great medicinal value.

Coconut (Narial)
Coconut is extensively usea in many Indian sweets and savouries. Buy a coconut, which contains a lot of water inside. Break open in two. Grate the coconut with a special grater or separate the kernel from the shell by heating and then grating with a grater or in a food processor Coconut is used either in a grated form or as a coconut milk extract.

Dessicated Coconut (Khaman)
Tiny dry, flakes of the coconut. This is easily available at the grocers and is mainly used in preparing cakes, biscuits and puddings. Always preserve dessicated coconut in an airtight box and store in the refrigerator.

Coriander (Dhania)
Coriander leaves (dhania) forms an aromatic herb similar to parsley. Its leaves and tender stems are used in cooking and also as garnish. Coriander seeds (dhania) are whole and in powdered form, are commonly used in many spice mixtures, savouries vegetable dishes and pickles.

Herbs & Spices

Cumin seeds (Jeera)
Small, aromatic seeds which give off additional aroma when roasted or added to hot oil. Cumin seeds, whole or in powdered form and commonly used in Indian cooking.

Curry leaves (Meetha Neem or Karipatta)
Aromatic leaves are used fresh in many Indian dishes. Like Bay leaves, they are added for their flavour and set aside while eating.

DILL (Suwa bhaji)
Dill is a feathery succulent of the parsley family. The leaves can be used fresh or dried and have a mild caraway-like flavour. It is used in many vegetable dishes, salads and soups.

Fennel seeds
Fennel seeds are used for flavouring many vegetable dishes and pickles. These seeds are also roasted and eaten after meals as a mouth freshener.

Fenugreek seeds (Methi)
They are used (whole or broken) in pickles and for flavouring vegetable and curries. But they are used sparingly as they have a bitter taste. Fenugreek leaves are used as a vegetable and also in preparing Indian style breads.

Ginger (Adrak)
It is used in many Indian savoury dishes. Scrape off the skin before grating or chopping very finely. It can also be crushed in an electric wet grinder. One can store ginger placed in a paper bag, in the refrigerator for a long time. Ginger is also dried and powdered. This powder is used in preparing confectionery and biscuits.

Garlic (Lasun)
This has a strong smell with segments known as cloves. Garlic has considerable medicinal value. It is thought to purify the blood and reduce cholesterol. It enhances the flavour of curries, chutneys and pickles. It is also available in powdered form.

Groundnuts or Peanuts
These brown nuts are roasted and rubbed over with a coarse cloth to remove their skins, then stored in air-tight bottles. They are used in a coarse, powdered form for many savoury dishes. Sweets are also prepared with them.

Mace (Javintri)
The outer orange coloured membrane of the nutmeg. This is powdered and used sparingly in sweets as well as savoury dishes, as it has a very strong flavour.

Molasses (Jaggery or Gur)
This is made of sugarcane juice and is found in a light yellow to brownish colour in lump form. Store in an air-tight bottle. It is used for sweetening and has more nutritional value than sugar.

Mustard Seeds (Rye)
These are tiny, round, reddish-brown or black seeds. They are used whole, broken, as a paste or in powdered form. Mustard paste has a most pungent taste.

Nigella Seeds
These are tiny black seeds with a distinctive flavour. They are used for (Kalongi or onion seeds) flavouring some vegetarian snacks and pickles.

Nutmeg (Jaiphal)
Its hard outer kernel is broken open to remove the nut-like, brown, pungent smelling seed inside. This is powdered and used sparingly in sweets and savoury dishes.

Pistachios (Pista)
These nuts are available either whole, with hard shells or shelled. They are green with a reddish brown thin skin. Roasted and salted, they can be used as a snack. Pistachios taste good in ice creams and many other sweet dishes.

Pomegranate Seeds (Anardana)
Pomegranate seeds are dried and stored for use as a spice. The powdered seeds give a nice tangy flavour as well as a dark colour to the dish.

Poppy Seeds (Khus Khus)
These are tiny, cream coloured seeds and are used whole or made into a paste. They are popular for use in sweet as well as savoury dishes like curries and snacks.

Sabja Seeds (Tukmaria)
These tiny black seeds are thought to have a cooling effect on the stomach. They swell up on soaking and are commonly used in Falooda.

Saffron (Kesar)
Saffron is the most expensive spice. It imparts a pleasing flavour as well as a golden yellow colouring. Saffron is the dried stigma and part of the style, of the complete saffron flower. It is available in a powdered form also. It is used for colouring and flavouring pullaos, sweets and puddings. It makes very pleasant cold drinks too.

Rose water (Gulab jal)
A clear liquid, distilled from fresh rose petals, it is readily available in bottles. It is used in small quantities for flavouring sweets and cold drinks. Pink, fragrant, fresh rose petals are also used to garnish certain Indian sweets.

Sesame seeds (Til)
The beige unpolished sesame seeds are better for use in recipes than the white polished ones. This gives a very pleasant nutty flavour on roasting. A black variety is also available.

Tamarind (Imli)
This is the fruit of the tamarind tree. Its fresh tender green pods, with their sharp sour taste. The ripe brown pods are cleaned of its brittle brown skin and hard seeds. Tamarind is used for many vegetables, pulses, snacks sauces and chutneys.

Turmeric (Haldi)
Turmeric is a root with a bright yellow colour. Fresh root, chopped and mixed with lemon juice and salt, is used as a pickle. Turmeric root is dried and powdered for use as a spice. It is commonly used in many vegetarian dishes.

Vanilla
An essence sold sometimes as dried pods but more easily available as a bottled liquid. It is mainly used to flavour puddings, cakes and milk shakes.

Walnuts (Akhrot)
A popular nut, it is sold whole in its hard shell or shelled. They are excellent in salads, cakes, ice creams and other sweet dishes.

Savoury Dishes

Chips Dhokra

Ingredients:

1 cup chana dal
1 cup urad dal
2 cups of rice
½ a cup oil
10 grated green chillies
1 inch piece ginger crushed
2 cloves of garlic crushed
salt to taste
½ tsp turmeric powder
pinch of asafoetida
1 tsp cumin powder
½ a cup green coriander leaves chopped
1½ cup yogurt
2 tsp sugar
1 tbsp sesame seeds
1 tsp eno

Method:

- Soak all three pulses separately for 4 hours.
- Now grind in the grinder with the yogurt adding water if necessary.
- Now add salt, turmeric powder and asafoetida.
- Mix well, cover and leave to ferment for 6 to 7 hours.
- In a large saucepan add 3 cups of water, bring to boil. Place a metal ring in the saucepan. Cover the lid of the pan with a piece of cloth so that the steam does not drop into the thali.
- Meanwhile add chillies, ½ a cup oil, sugar, cumin powder, garlic, ginger, coriander leaves, and sesame seeds to the mixture and mix very well.
- Spread a little oil in a thali and place this on the metal ring in the saucepan.
- In a small pan place about 1 ½ cups of the mixture and add 1 tsp eno and mix well. Now pour this mixture into the thali and steam for 10 to 15 minutes, covering the big pan with the lid.
- Remove the dhokra from the pan and repeat the process for the rest of the mixture. Once the dhokra are cool, cut into chips.
- Either eat hot or temper with sesame seed and asafoetida (hing) and enjoy with green chutney.

Moong Dal Kachori

Ingredients for Kachori:

½ lb moong dal
1 tsp cinnamon & clove powder
½ lb peas crushed
1 tsp cumin powder
3 green chillies
½ tsp ginger paste
1 cup coriander leaves chopped
1 tsp cumin powder
½ cup grated coconut
sugar and salt to taste
1 lemon
1 green mango grated
½ a cup oil
3 tbsp fennel powder

Ingredients for Dough:

¾ cup oil for plain flour
3 cups plain flour
pinch of asafoetida
1 tbsp semolina

Method:

- Wash and soak dal for three hours.
- Heat ½ cup of oil in a large saucepan.
- Temper cumin seeds and add asafoetida.
- Now add dal with peas and one cup of water. Cook for 5 mins.
- Add rest of ingredients and form small balls.
- Knead flour with one tbsp semolina and ¾ cup oil.
- Use warm water to knead the flour and dough to produce a soft dough.
- Take a little dough in the palm and flatten.
- Put the ball in the centre and cover kachori with the dough.
- Place the kachoris on a floured plate
- Now deep fry at a medium temperature.
- Tastes very nice with sweet chutney.
- You may freeze kachories and samosas, fry for one minute, cool and freeze.

Red, Green and Sweet Chutney

RED CHUTNEY
Ingredients:

1 red capsicum
1 carrot
1 raw mango
2 cloves garlic
1 tsp cumin powder
3 tbsp tomato sauce
1 tbsp jaggery
1 tsp red chilli powder

Method:

• Wash clean and liquidize all the
  above ingredients.

GREEN CHUTNEY
Ingredients:

1 raw mango
6 green chillies
1 bunch of coriander leaves
½ a bunch mint
1 tsp cumin
3 tsp sugar and 1 tsp salt
2 tbsp sev or gathia
3 to 4 cloves garlic
1" ginger

Method:

• Wash clean and liquidize all the
  above ingredients

SWEET CHUTNEY
Ingredients:

1 pkt dates
1½ tbsp tamarind
1 tbsp jaggery
1 tsp cumin powder
1 tsp red chilli powder
salt according to taste

Method:

• Boil dates, jaggery and tamarind.
• Sieve the juice, add the rest of the
  ingredients and liquidize.
• May decorate with little green
  chopped coriander.

Falafal

Ingredients for pakoda:
1 bowl channa-gram dal
1 chopped onion
1 tsp cumin powder
2 cloves crushed garlic
6 green chillies chopped
1½" ginger crushed
1 ½ tsp salt & 1 tsp sugar
2 tbsp gram flour
1 tsp coriander and cumin powder
2 pinches of eno
2 tbsp chopped coriander leaves
pinch of turmeric powder
oil for frying

Method:
- Soak chana dal for 4 hours.
- Drain the rest of the dal and liquidize, with a little water. Make sure mixture is not watery.
- Add the above spices to the dal and mix well.
- Heat some oil in a deep frying pan.
- Take 1 tbsp of the mixture and roll round in the palm of your hand.
- Now deep fry till golden brown. (these are the pakoda)

Ingredients for nan:
3 bowls self raising flour (or plain flour)
If using the plain flour add 1 tsp bicarbonate of soda.
1 tsp salt
1 tsp sugar
1 pkt yeast
½ a cup yogurt
3 tbsp oil

Method:
- In a large bowl place the above ingredients and knead the flour to form a soft dough.
- Knead for 10 minutes and cover with a wet cloth. Keep covered for 4 hours till double in size. Heat the tawa and roll nan oblong.
- Cook on one side and put under the grill or use a tawa for cooking on both sides.
- Now cover with cloth and keep aside.

Falafal salad Ingredients:
1 small cabbage, 1 onion, 1 cucumber, 1 tomato, lettuce and cheese.
Make a slit on the side of nan, spread red chutney, add 2 pakodas, with green chutney, cheese and chopped salad.

Paneer Samosa

Ingredients:

8 pts of milk
1 tsp citric acid or lemon juice
1 lb peas
2 onions chopped
½ cup oil
1 tsp cumin seeds
8 green chilli crushed
1" ginger crushed
1 cup coriander leaves chopped finely
1 tbsp cumin powder
2½ tsp salt
pinch of asafoetida

Method:

• Boil milk and dissolve citric acid.
• Add to the boiling milk; the milk will curdle. Strain through a muslin cloth.
• Heat oil and add cumin and asafoetida.
• Add onion and cook till brown.
• Add peas, chillies and ginger paste.
• Add salt & cook mixture for 2 mins.
• Now add paneer, cumin powder, salt and coriander leaves.
• Remove from the heat.

Ingredients: Samosa pastry
1 lb plain flour
½ a tsp citric powder
½ a cup oil
1 tsp salt
oil for brushing and frying and warm water.

Method: (Pastry)

• Make soft dough with the above ingredients.
• Make equal balls. Roll each ball into round roti.
• Brush with oil and sprinkle plain flour.
• Now roll another roti and brush oil and sprinkle flour. Put this roti on top of the first one.
• Make 6 to 7 roties pilling on top of previous roti.
• Now roll a big roti from the pile.
• Cook this roti on a tawa at a low temperature, on both sides.
• Now separate each roti and cover with a damp cloth. Cut each roti in half.
• Bring both ends to the centre to make a pocket.
• Put in the above filling and press the top.
• Make paste using water and flour, cook till it becomes sticky.
• Use this paste to seal the top of the samosa.
• Prepare all the samosas and deep fry till golden.

Sweet Potato and Potato Handwo

Ingredients:

1½ lb sweet potatoes, 1 lb potatoes
1½ lb green peas, 2" crushed ginger
13 green chillies crushed
3 cloves garlic crushed
oil to temper, 3 pinches of asafoetida
½ tsp black pepper powder
1 pinch of turmeric powder
2 tbsp desiccated coconut
1 lemon juice
3 tsp sugar, salt according to taste
2 tsp cumin powder
1½ cups chopped coriander leaves
2 tbsp sesames seeds
1½ tsp mustard seeds
1 piece of cinnamon, 3 cloves
½ tsp fennel seeds
1½ cup gram flour and curry leaves

Method:

- Crush peas.
- Steam potatoes and sweet potatoes separately.
- Mash both.
- Add 2 tbsp oil to both the potatoes.
- Now add crushed ginger, chillies, salt, black pepper and coriander leaves and mix well.
- In a pan heat 3 tbsp oil and add cinnamon, cloves, cumin and asafoetida.
- Add peas to the above tempered oil.
- Add salt, ginger, chillies garlic and sugar.
- Mix well and cook for five mins
- Once cooked add fennel, lemon juice, cumin powder and chopped coriander leaves.
- Add coconut and remove from the heat.
- Oil the baking tray and spread a layer of potato mixture.
- Top up with a layer of peas.
- Now layer with sweet potatoes.
- Make a thin batter of gram flour, with warm water.
- Just add salt and turmeric powder.
- Now spread this batter on top of all the layers.
- Heat the oven to gas mark 4.
- In another pan heat ½ a cup oil and add mustard, cumin, sesame, pinch of asafoetida and curry leaves.
- Spread this tempered oil on the layers and bake in the oven for 1 hour.

Mushroom Curry and Bhakhari

Ingredients:

500 gm mushrooms
3 cloves crushed garlic
2 small chopped onions
1" crushed ginger
3 ripe tomatoes
5 crushed green chillies
1 tsp salt
½ cup oil
¼ tsp turmeric powder
1 tsp cumin
2 tsp coriander and cumin powder
and pinch of asafoetida/hing
Few cloves and 2 pieces of cinnamon
chopped coriander leaves.

Method:

• Wash mushrooms and slice.
• Heat the oil in a large pan.
• Add cloves, cinnamon, cumin, asafoetida and chopped onion.
• Fry onion till pink in colour.
• Now add crushed tomatoes and the rest of the ingredients except for the mushrooms.
• Cook for two minutes and then add mushrooms.
• Cook on high heat so that all the water evaporates.
• Once the water is reduced, cook with lid on for ten mins.
• Sprinkle chopped coriander leaves and enjoy with paratha or bhakhari.

Chilli Mogo (Hot Cassava)

Ingredients:

1lb mogo
2 hot chillis cut into small pieces
8 garlic cloves crushed
1 ½ tsp red chilli powder
½ red capsicum sliced
½ green capsicum thinly sliced
1 can chopped tomatoes
1 ½ tsp sugar
1 tsp soya sauce
1 tsp lemon juice
1 ½ tsp salt
2 spring onions sliced
1 tbsp coriander leaves for
garnishing
oil

Method:

- If the cassava is frozen, soak in hot water for 20 minutes.
- Now boil mogo with 1 tsp salt and then cut into chips, when cold.
- Fry all the chips.
- In a pan put 2 tbsp oil and temper the garlic.
- Add tomatoes, soya sauce, chopped chilli, salt, sugar, lemon juice, red chilli powder, red and green capsicums and mogo chips.
- Stir well and serve.
- Garnish with coriander leaves.

Vada Pav

Ingredients for filling:

2 lb potatoes
2 tsps sugar
7 green chillies crushed
½ cup fresh chopped coriander
1" ginger crushed
1 onion finely chopped
juice of 1 lemon
1 tsp cumin
1 tsp cumin powder
2 tbsps oil
1½ tsps salt
pinch of asafoetida

Ingredients for batter:

1½ bowls gram flour
1 pinch bicarbonate soda
1 tsp salt
½ tsp cumin powder
2 pinches of turmeric powder
½ cup fresh chopped coriander
1 pinch asafoetida

Method:

- Wash and boil the potatoes. When ready, skin and mash them.
- Heat oil in a saucepan, add cumin and fry the onions until pink in colour. Then add the mash, ginger, chillies and the rest of the above ingredients. Form large balls.
- Add warm water to the gram flour and add all the above ingredients of the batter to make a smooth batter.
- Heat oil in a frying pan. When ready, dip the potato balls into the batter and deep-fry everything.

Dry Chutney

- Crush 12 cloves of garlic with red chilli powder and spread in a tray to dry.
- Chop 2 onions and add gram flour, salt, red chilli powder and cumin and mix. Add water only if required. Then fry the pakoras in oil. When cool grind them and mix with the garlic chutney.
- Spread the dry chutney on one side of the bun, put the potato vada on top, close with the other half of the bun and serve.

Vegetable Burger

Ingredients:

1 cup kidney beans
1 cup garbanzo (chickpeas)
1 carrot finely chopped
1 bowl peas
1 bowl sweetcorn
1 bowl breadcrumbs
2 tbsp wheat flour
2 tbsp sesame seeds
2 tbsp soya sauce
7 to 8 crushed green chillies
2 cloves garlic
1 piece ginger crush
salt according to taste
1 tsp pepper

Method:

• Soak both the beans separately over night.
• Next day cook the beans and mash.
• Add chopped vegetables to the beans.
• Form burgers and coat in the breadcrumbs.
• Shallow fry in the frying pan on both sides till golden brown.
• Serve with the lettuce, cucumber, onion, tomatoes etc.
• Make your own topping and enjoy with the burger buns.
• You can freeze burgers and use later.

Cocktail Pizza

Ingredients:

The base:
1½ bowl self raising flour
1 pkt yeast
3 tbsp oil
1 tsp salt
1 tsp sugar
1 tsp cumin powder
luke warm water

The filling:
2 tins tomatoes
2 tbsp tomato paste
1 tsp salt
1½ tsp sugar
½ tsp pepper
1 onion cut into small pieces

2 cloves garlic
4 curry leaves
1 tsp mixed herbs
2 tbsp oil

The topping:
2 pkts cheese grated
1 red and 1 green capsicum sliced
2 onions sliced
½ tin corn
6 mushrooms sliced

Method:

- Knead flour with the above base ingredients using luke warm water.
- Cover and leave for 4 hours.
- For the filling, heat the oil and fry the onion.
- Add garlic tomatoes, salt, sugar and curry leaves and cook to form a thick sauce.
- Now add herbs, pepper and tomato paste.
- Mix well and take off the heat.
- Roll big rotti and cut cocktail size pizza.
- Top with desired toppings and bake in the oven at gas mark 4 to 5 for 15 minutes.

Masala Dhosa

Ingredients:

3 cups rice
1 cup urad dal without skin
1 tsp salt
oil

Stuffing:

1 ½ lb potatoes
1 lb onion
1" ginger crushed
1 tsp red chilli powder
½ cup chopped coriander leaves
1 ½ tsp salt
¼ tsp turmeric powder
2 tsp coriander and cumin powder
mustard, cumin and asafoetida/hing
to temper

Method:

- Wash the pulses twice and soak separately.
- Now liquidize separately and then mix together.
- Keep for the whole night to ferment.
- Next day add salt.
- Ensure you have a thin batter.

Method:

- Heat ¾ cup of oil and add mustard seeds, cumin and asafoetida.
- Now add potatoes and all the above stuffing ingredients.
- Cook on low temperature until cooked.
- Garnish with coriander leaves when ready

Method to make Masala Dhosa

- Heat a large non-stick frying pan.
- Rub water and oil on it.
- Stir the dhosa batter thoroughly.
- Now spread ½ a cup batter on the frying pan and quickly spread round with a small stainless steel bowl, or with the help of a big round spoon.
- Pour a little oil round the dhosa.
- Dhosa will be ready when the side will start lifting up.
- Turn dhosa and put a little potato curry in the middle.
- Cover the filling with both the sides of dhosa.
- Serve with coconut chutney, and sambhar.

Sambhar

Ingredients:

1 bowl tuverdal
1 small potato diced
1 small aubergines diced
1 carrot diced
1 onion diced
2 drumsticks cut into 3"
1 tsp turmeric powder
few curry leaves
2 tsp salt
1 tsp dal masala
2 cloves crushed garlic
3 tbsp oil
1 piece ginger
4 mild chillies
3 tomatoes chopped
½ tsp mustard, cumin &

asafoetida
½ cup chopped
coriander
1 tbsp sugar

Idli:
1 bowl urad dal
2 bowls rice
1 tsp salt
eno

Method for Sambhar and Idli:

- (Sambhar) Boil tuverdal with 8 cups of water, 1 tsp salt, until cooked.
- Heat the oil and add mustard, cumin and curry leaves with asafoetida. Once tempered add onion and cook till brown.
- Add tomatoes. After 5 minutes add all the vegetables.
- Add all the spices and boiled dal.
- Garnish with coriander leaves and eat with idli.
- (Idli) Soak urad dal and rice separately overnight, wash dal and grind in the grinder separately and now mix together.
- Leave to ferment for 7 hours and then add salt.
- Place some of the mixture in a seperate bowl, add half tsp eno and fill an oiled Idly stand with the mixture. (Can be made in a steamer also.)
- Steam for 10-15 minutes.

Chana Dal Kachori

Ingredients:

½ lb chana dal
½ lb peas crushed
green chillies and ginger
paste
1 tsp cumin powder
sugar and salt to taste
1 green mango grated
3 tbsp fennel powder
3 cup plain flour
1 tbsp semolina
1 tsp cinnamon & clove
powder
1 tsp cumin powder
1 cup coriander leaves

chopped
½ a cup grated coconut
1 lemon
½ a cup oil
¾ cup oil for plain flour
pinch of asafoetida

Method:

- Wash and soak dal for three hours.
- In a pan, put oil for seasoning. Add cumin seeds and asafoetida.
- Now add dal and one cup of water.
- When half cooked then add peas.
- Add all above ingredients and mix well and make small balls.
- Knead flour with one tbsp semolina and ¾ cup oil with warm water.
- Dough should be droopy.
- Take a little dough in the palm and spread it.
- Put the ball in the centre and cover kachori from all sides.
- In a tray sprinkle flour and put in all the rolled balls.
- Now deep fry at medium temperature.
- Tastes very nice with sweet chutney.

Khandvi

Ingredients:

1 cup gram flour
mustard, cumin and asafoetida
1 cup yogurt
¼ tsp sugar
2 cups of water
oil
4 crushed chillies
½ cup chopped coriander leaves
½ tsp salt
¼ cup desiccated coconut
½ tsp turmeric powder
1 thick plastic sheet
1 green chilli cut into pieces
1 tsp sesame seeds

Method:

• First make butter milk by adding 2 cups of water to 1 cup of yogurt.
• Now add gram flour to the butter milk.
• Add salt, turmeric powder, green chillies and sugar.
• Mix very well and put on the gas at low temperature.
• Keep stirring all the time.
• Once the batter becomes thick, spread a little on a work surface. Leave to cool and try to peel off. If it peels off easily, the mixture is ready.
• Now put this batter at the top of the plastic sheet and quickly spread evenly and thin.
• Use flat spoon to spread.

• Use your palm to spread smoothly if you wish and leave to cool.
• Now cut about 3" strips.
• Roll each strip into the thickness you desire. The thickness should be roughly the thickness of sausages.
• Keep rolling and cutting the strips.
• Arrange in a dish neatly.
• Sprinkle chopped coriander and coconut on it.
• Heat the oil and add mustard, sesame seeds, green chillies, cumin, curry leaves and asafoetida.
• Pour over the khandvi with a spoon.

Khasta Kachori

Ingredients:

1 bowl moong dal
1" crushed ginger
1 tsp salt
2 tsp sugar
1 tsp red chilli powder
1 cup chopped coriander leaves
1 tsp salt
2 tbsp amchur powder or raw mango grated
5 tbsp oil
1 tsp cumin
¼ tsp asafoetida
½ tsp cinnamon, cloves and black pepper powder

Yogurt ingredients:

1 bowl yogurt
4 crushed green chillies
½ tsp cumin
pinch of sugar
thin sev (gram flour)

Pastry ingredients:

¾ cup oil
oil for frying
1 lb plain flour
1 tsp salt

Method:

- Soak dal for 3 hours and wash.
- In a pan put oil and temper dal with cumin seeds and asafoetida.
- Add ¼ cup water or as required to cook dal.
- Add salt ginger and green chillies and let it cook. It should be dry.
- Before taking it off the heat add red chilli powder, sugar, grated mango, cinnamon, cloves and black pepper and half the green coriander.
- Mix well and take it off the heat.
- Knead plain flour with oil and water to make a firm dough.
- Roll small puri and fill with the above mixture.
- Bring all the ends together and just roll once or press with hand.
- Deep fry in the oil at a very low temperature till golden brown.
- While serving make a little hole and add a little yogurt, and sev and garnish with coriander leaves and serve.

Green Chevdo (Nadiad No Lilo Chevdo)

Ingredients:

1 bowl chana dal
(gram-dal)
1 bowl cashew nuts
½ bowl almonds
½ bowl peanuts
2 lbs potatoes
1 cup coriander leaves
1 ½ tsp salt to taste
1 lemon juice
oil to fry
½ cup sugar
2 tbsp red chilli powder
½ tbsp turmeric powder
pieces of green chilli
1 cup desiccated coconut
few curry leaves

pinch of red and yellow
food colouring
thin slices of green
mango
cumin seeds and
asafoetida

Method:

- Soak chana dal overnight and strain and let it dry.
- Grate potatoes and deep fry till crispy and fry chana dal till crispy.
- Mix potatoes and chana dal with salt, turmeric powder and chilli powder.
- Fry cashew nuts, almonds, peanuts, pieces of green chillies and curry leaves and add to the above.
- Make sugar syrup with ½ bowl water and mix with the above chevda and also add lemon juice.
- Garnish with coconut, coriander leaves and mango slices.
- This cannot be kept for too long, so consume within a week.

Cornflour Dhebra

Ingredients:

1 lb fine cornflour
1 bowl wholemeal flour
½ bowl rice flour
½ cup oil
1 bowl yogurt
1 tsp eno
2 bunches of fresh methi (fenugreek leaves) finely chopped
3 tsp salt
6 tsp sugar
1 tsp ground cumin
2" piece of ginger grated
10 green chillies crushed
1 tbsp turmeric powder
1 tbsp dhanajeeru (cumin & coriander powder)
1 tbsp ajmo
½ cup sesame
½ tsp asafoetida
6 cloves garlic crushed
oil for frying

Method:

- Mix all three flours and add all the above ingredients.
- Knead dough with yogurt and leave over night.
- Make small balls of equal size.
- Place a dry thin cloth on a floured surface and sprinkle a few drops of water.
- On this cloth place 5 balls and press each ball lightly either with your hand or the bottom of a small bowl.
- Deep fry until both sides are brown.
- This dhebra is convenient while travelling.

Masaledar Dal Vaata (Muthia)

Ingredients:

2 cups moongdal
½ cup gourd dudhi
1" crushed ginger
7 green chilli crushed
1 clove garlic crushed
1 tsp chilli powder
½ cup chopped coriander
pinch of asafoetida
pinch of baking powder
1 tsp salt
1 tsp sugar

Method:

- Wash moong dal and soak for 3 hours.
- Liquidize.
- Grate gourd and mix with dal.
- Now add the above ingredients except asafoetida.
- Mix well and make long vaata (like thick sausages).
- Steam this vaata for ¾ of an hour and eat hot with sunflower oil, or you may temper in the oil.
- Cut into round pieces.
- Heat oil and add tsp cumin seeds and a pinch of asafoetida.
- Now add cut vaata to this and cook at a medium temperature for 10 mins.
- Garnish with coriander leaves.
- You may sprinkle a little desiccated coconut.

Rus Fulwadi

Ingredients:

1 bowl gram flour
250g potatoes
3 tomatoes
1 cup yogurt
grated coconut
chopped coriander leaves
salt according to taste
sweet chutney
½ tsp black coarse pepper
pinch of garam masala (optional)
1" grated ginger
5 chopped green chillies
1 tsp sugar
oil for frying

Method:

- Boil potatoes, remove the skin and mash.
- Add salt, sugar, ginger, chillies, yogurt and gram flour and mix well.
- Make small balls the size of a marble.
- Deep fry.
- Cut tomatoes into slices and arrange in a dish.
- In the middle arrange all the rasfulwadi (mountain shape).
- Sprinkle sweet chutney, coconut and green coriander.
- Enjoy with a drink!

Bread Vada

Ingredients:

1½ lb potatoes
¼ lb peas
1 cup coriander leaves chopped
1 white bread
10 raisins
10 green chillies crushed
1"ginger crushed
1 tsp cumin powder
1 cup grated coconut
1 tsp butter
1 tsp sugar and 1 tsp salt to taste
juice of 2 lemons

Method:

• Boil potato and mash.
• Saute peas in butter.
• Mix potato and peas and add all the above ingredients except bread.
• Cut the crust and side of the bread and wet with little water.
• Press the slice with your hand and put in the filling of potato and peas.
• Shape into round balls.
• Deep fry at a low temperature till crispy.
• Enjoy with a any chutney or ketchup.

Moora Na Paratha

Ingredients:

1 big moora (white radish)
1lb wheat flour
1 tsp ajmo
1½ tsp salt
3 tbsp oil
1 tsp red chilli powder
1 tsp cumin powder
oil and ghee for frying

Method:

- Grate radish and add salt.
- Leave for ten minutes and squeeze the water out.
- In a large bowl add wheat flour and all the masala.
- Add grated radish and add 3 tbsp. of oil and mix well.
- Softly knead flour and make parathas.
- Fry in the pan with both ghee and oil.
- Cook on both sides.
- Eat with yogurt, tea, or with ripe mango.

Sev Puri

Ingredients:

½ pkt tamarind
1 bowl plain flour
1 pkt dates
½ cup mint leaves
6 green chillies
3 cloves
3 cinnamon
1" ginger
½ tsp cumin
1 cup coriander leaves
1 tsp fennel
1 tsp black pepper
pinch salt according to taste
3 boiled potatoes
thin sev

½ tbsp dry coriander seeds
¼ cup semolina
1 bowl yogurt
oil
½ tsp turmeric powder

Method:

- Boil dates and tamarind. Strain the mixture to form a thick syrup.
- Crush ginger, chillies, coriander leaves, black pepper, fennel, coriander seeds, cinnamon, cloves, salt, cumin and mint leaves.
- Add this to the thick syrup.
- Mix semolina and plain flour, add oil and knead to form a firm dough.
- Now roll a big thin chapatti and with a small round cutter cut small puris like pani puri.
- Fry in hot oil until crispy. (You can buy puris from Indian savoury shops.)
- Peel the boiled potatoes and cut into small pieces.
- Temper with a little oil adding salt and little turmeric powder.
- Remove from the heat.
- Keep puris on the plate and put potatoes on the top with a little sev on it. Put 2 tsp of tamarind chutney on.
- Add salt and coriander leaves to the yogurt and put on top of the puris.

Pattis

Ingredients:

2 lb potatoes
1 lb peas
2 tbsp varanga flour or cornflour
8 green chillies crushed
1" ginger grated
3 tbsp desiccated coconut
½ cup chopped coriander leaves
1 tsp salt
2 tsp sugar
1 tsp cumin powder
½ lemon juice
½ cup oil
pinch of asafoetida

Method:

• Boil potatoes, skin and mash.
• Add salt and varanga flour.
• Mix well.
• Crush peas.
• Heat oil, add cumin and asafoetida.
• Now add peas.
• Add all the above masala (ingredients) and cook till done.
• Lastly add lemon and sugar and remove from the heat.
• Once cool make small balls.
• Take mashed potato in the palm and spread like puri.
• Now put the ball of peas in the middle and cover all the sides.
• Heat oil in the pan and deep fry all the pattis until golden brown.
• Serve hot with any chutney.

Powa Potato

Ingredients:

1 lb potatos
1 cup powa (puffed rice)
½ cup oil
1 tbsp lemon juice
½ cup chopped
coriander leaves
1 tbsp peanuts
1 tsp cumin
¾ tsp salt
½ tsp turmeric powder
2 green chillies cut into
pieces
5 green chillies crushed
1" ginger crushed

2 tsp sugar
few curry leaves
pinch of asafoetida

Method:

- Skin and cut potatoes into small cubes.
- Wash powa and strain all the water.
- In a pan heat oil and temper with cumin curry leaves, peanuts and pinch a of asafoetida.
- Now add potatoes, salt turmeric powder, ginger paste and chilli paste.
- Stir softly and cook at a low temperature till potatoes are cooked.
- Now add powa, lemon juice and sugar, cut chilli and coriander leaves.
- Serve hot.

Ragda Pattis

Ingredients:

1 bowl dry peas
1 chopped onion
2 tomatoes chopped
½ tsp turmeric
powder
2" pc ginger –
crushed
2 tsps sugar
1 tsp red chilli
powder
Oil
½ tsp salt to taste
1 tsp cumin
6-7 crushed green
chillies
Date – Tamarind
juice

Pattis:

1 kg potatoes
½ lb green peas
2 tbsps cornflour
on 4 slices of
bread
1 tsp salt to
taste
5 green crushed
chillies
1" crushed
ginger
1 lemon - juiced

Method:

- Wash and soak the dry peas for 4 hours. Change water and add 1 tsp salt and pressure-cook for 20 minutes.
- Heat oil in a saucepan, add cumin and asafoetida then add chopped onions and cook until light brown in colour.
- Add tomatoes and rest of the ingredients and cook until the oil separates from the sauce. Then add the date – tamarind juice and let it simmer for a few minutes.
- Finally add the boiled peas. Mix and leave for 5 minutes and remove from heat.

Pattis:

- Boil the potatoes, skin and mash. To it add 1 tsp salt to cornflour or bread.
- Heat oil in a saucepan and add crushed peas. Add ½ tsp salt, sugar, ginger paste, chilli paste, lemon and coriander. Mix thoroughly and make small balls. Take some mashed potato and flatten.
- Put one ball of peas and cover all over. Do the same with all the balls. Flatten them and deep fry in very hot oil.
- Place pattis on a plate (1 or 2), pour Ragdo over it and then pour date – tamarind chutney, yogurt and chopped onion and serve hot.

Semolina Dhokra

Ingredients:

1 bowl semolina (250gm)
½ cup gram flour
1 bowl yogurt
7 green chillies grated
1" ginger chopped
1½ tsp salt
4 tsp sugar
¼ tsp turmeric powder
1 tbsp lemon juice
½ cup oil
½ cup coriander chopped
1 tsp cumin powder
1 tsp eno

Method:

• Mix semolina and gram flour in a pan.
• Mix all the above ingredients and make soft batter in warm water.
• Boil water in a steamer.
• Grease stainless steal plate to make dhokra.
• Take enough batter to fill the plate and add 1tsp eno.
• Stir quickly and pour onto the plate.
• Now steam for 15 to 20 minutes.
• Remove from the steamer and cut into squares.
• You may eat hot as it is or you may temper in oil using mustard, sesame seeds and a pinch of asafoetida.
• Garnish with fresh coriander leaves.

Gobi Na Rasa Wala Muthia

Ingredients:

½ lb cabbage grated
1 tsp turmeric powder
1 aubergine chopped
2 tsp salt
1 onion
1 tbsp coriander and cumin powder (Dhana Jeeru)
8 beans or valor/guvar beans chopped
1 bowl cooked rice or hotchpotch
½ cup fresh fenugreek leaves
1½ bowl gram flour

1" crushed ginger
½ cup whole wheat flour
10 crushed green chillies
1 tsp cumin
5 cloves of garlic crushed
pinch of asafoetida
1½ bowl yogurt
½ a cup oil
½ a cup chopped coriander
2 pieces of cinnamon
3 cloves
¼ tsp sugar

Method:

- Cut aubergine.
- In a big bowl grate cabbage and onion.
- Add cooked rice.
- Add gram flour and wheat flour with ginger, garlic, green chilli, salt, dhana jeeru, turmeric powder and ½ cup oil.
- Mix all and form small muthia.
- Keep aside.
- Heat oil in a pan.
- Add cinnamon and cloves.
- Temper with cumin seeds and asafoetida.

- Now add aubergine.
- Add garlic, ginger green chilli, salt and a little turmeric powder.
- Stir well.
- Make thin buttermilk and add this to the vegetables.
- Keep stirring till it starts to boil.
- Now add muthia.
- Let it boil at a medium temperature.
- The gravy will become thick.
- Add ¼ tsp sugar and garnish with coriander leaves.
- Serve hot.

Semolina Handwo

Ingredients:

1lb coarse semolina
½ cup oil
1 ½ cups yogurt
1 large potato
1 small piece of cabbage
3 grated onions
10 green chillies crushed
2" ginger crushed
3 cloves crushed garlic
1 tbsp cumin powder
2 tsp turmeric powder
2 tsp coriander and
cumin powder
¼ tsp turmeric powder

3 tsp salt
7 tsp sugar
1 ½ tsp eno
1 cup coriander leaves
1 lemon juice
¾ cup oil
½ tsp mustard seeds
1 tsp cumin seeds
2 tbsp sesame seeds
two pinches asafoetida
for tempering

Method:

- Shred potato, onion and cabbage in a large pan.
- Add all the above ingredients with eno, yogurt and oil
- Heat the oven at gas mark 6 180°.
- Temper mustard, cumin, sesame seeds and asafoetida and add to the above mixture.
- Spread in the baking tray and bake in the oven for one hour at gas mark 6, 180°.

Palakh Paneer Na Gunja

Ingredients:

1 bunch palakh-spinach
½ lb cabbage
½ lb carrots
¼ lb paneer fresh
½ cup desiccated coconut
1 tsp cumin
pinch of asafoetida
1 lb plain flour
1 tsp chilli powder
1 tsp salt
pinch garam masala
1 cup coriander leaves
oil

Method:

- Boil spinach and liquidize.
- Knead plain flour with a little oil, salt and spinach.
- Grate cabbage and carrots.
- In a pan put little oil and temper with cumin seeds.
- Add cabbage and carrots.
- Now add chilli powder, panneer, desiccated coconut and garam masala.
- Mix well. Add coriander leaves.
- Now form equal balls from the dough to make the chapattis.
- Roll one chapatti and spread the above vegetable mixture on it.
- Cover this chapatti with another plain chapatti.
- Press from all the sides, and make a design using the thumb and first finger. Prepare all gunjas like this.
- Deep fry all gunjas till light pink or shallow fry.
- Serve with yogurt or tomato soup.

Masala Makai Paneer

Ingredients:

7 corn on the cob (separate corn from one cob)
3 pints of milk for paneer
2 chopped onions
1 lb grated tomatoes
1 cup green coriander chopped (for garnish)
10 green chillies chopped
1 tbsp tomato purée
1 cup oil

¼ tsp cumin and asafoetida
1" piece ginger crushed
1 tsp turmeric powder
1 tsp chilli powder
1 tbsp desiccated coconut
2 tsp salt
1 tsp sugar
little lemon juice

Method:

- Boil milk.
- Put ½ a tsp citric acid in the milk to separate paneer.
- Drain and wash the paneer in cold water.
- Now put paneer in a cloth to drain all the water. The paneer should be dry.
- Cut 6 cobs into 1" pieces.
- Partly cook the corn with a little salt and turmeric powder.
- In a pan put oil and temper with cumin and asafoetida.
- Add onion and cook till brown.
- Add tomatoes and all the above ingredients.
- Stir well and boil till tomatoes are cooked.
- Add pieces of corn and separate corn.
- Now add paneer and cook till done.
- Garnish with coriander leaves.

Stuffed Chilli Bhajia

Ingredients:

1 lb long mild chillies
1 lb potatoes
1 lb gram flour
1 cup peas
½" crushed ginger
4 green chillies crushed
1 tsp cumin powder
1 tsp salt
1 cup chopped coriander leaves
1 tsp butter
1 tsp wheat flour
½ tsp eno
1 tsp salt for the batter

Method:

• Boil potatoes, skin and mash.
• Fry peas in the butter.
• Add mashed potato to peas.
• Add ginger, chilli, salt, cumin powder and coriander leaves.
• Mix well.
• Wash chillies and slice down one side.
• Fill with the potato/pea mixture.
• Make thick batter with gram flour and wheat flour using warm water.
• Add salt.
• Add ½ tsp Eno
• Dip the chillies in the batter and deep fry until golden brown.
• Enjoy with green chutney.

Vegetable Dhokra

Ingredients:

1 ½ cups rice
½ moong dhal
½ lb peas crushed
2 potatoes chopped
1 carrot chopped
12 green beans chopped
1 small onion chopped
1 tsp chilli, ginger, garlic paste
½ tsp salt and sugar to taste
½ tsp eno
3 tbsps oil
1 tsp mustard seeds
1 tsp sesame seeds
pinch of asafoetida

Method:

• Wash rice and soak overnight. Next day liquidize coarsely and add ½ tsp eno.
• Next day soak moong dhal for 2 hours then liquidize coarsely.
• Keep both separate. Add salt to both mixtures.
• In a saucepan heat oil and cumin seeds and asafoetida. Add onions and fry till pink in colour. Then add all the chopped vegetables, stir and then add all the above ingredients and let it cook.
• When ready remove from heat and keep aside.
• In a steamer, oil the idli stand and pour rice mixture into each compartment. Put the vegetable mixture in and then pour the moong mixture over it. Cover and let it cook for 15 minutes. (You can use the thali as well.)
• When all is ready, heat oil and add mustard seeds, asafoetida and sesame seeds with curry leaves and then garnish the dhokras. Serve with any chutney of your choice.

Stuffed whole Potato Pakoda

Ingredients:

1 kg small potatoes
6 cloves of garlic crushed
1 tbsp red chilli powder
1 cup chopped coriander
1 tbsp roasted cumin powder
1 green chilli crushed
½ tsp sugar
1 tbsp lemon juice
1 tbsp oil
1 ¼ tsp salt

Batter Ingredients:

½ kg gram flour
1 tsp salt
½ tsp turmeric
1 pinch baking powder
1 tsp cumin powder
pinch asafoetida
oil for frying

Method:

• Boil potatoes.
• Remove the skin and softly make four cuts on the top. Make sure the potato remains whole.
• Mix all the above ingredients and softly stuff all the potatoes.
• Keep aside.

Batter Method:
• Form a thin batter with water by mixing all the ingredients.
• Add all the above spices.
• Now dip each potato in the batter and fry until golden.

Methi Na Thepla and Suki Bhajia

Ingredients:

2 bowls wheat flour
½ bowl gram flour
¾ cup oil. 1 bunch
of fenugreek leaves
chopped
½ cup chopped corian-
der leaves, 1 tsp turmeric
powder. ½ tsp ajmo, oil
2" chopped ginger
8 green chilli crushed
6 cloves garlic crushed
1 tsp cumin powder
1 tbsp coriander, cumin
and dhana jeeru
1 ½ tsp salt
1 tbsp sesame seeds
2 pinches of asafoetida

Suki Bhajia:

1 lb potato
1 clove garlic
1" ginger
a few green chillies
crushed
1 tsp cumin
few curry leaves
4 tbsp oil mustard,
cumin and asafoetida for
tempering
1 tsp salt
½ tsp turmeric powder
½ cup chopped
coriander leaves

Method for Thepla:

• Mix the flour with the fenugreek leaves.
• Add the rest of the ingredients to the flour.
• Mix well, add warm water and form a soft dough.
• Now roll into chapattis and shallow fry in the frying pan on both sides till done.

Method for Bhajia:

• Skin potato and cut into cubes.
• Heat the oil and temper with cumin, mustard, curry leaves and asafoetida.
• Now add potatoes and all the above ingredients.
• Cover and cook on a low heat.
• Garnish with coriander leaves.

Methi Na Gota

Ingredients:

2 bowls gram flour
1 tsp wholemeal flour
2 bunches methi leaves, chopped
1 potato, chopped
7 chillies, finely crushed
1 tbsp cumin powder
1" ginger, crushed
1 cup coriander leaves, chopped
½ tsp black pepper
½ tsp eno
½ tsp sugar

2 tsp salt
1 tbsp sesame seeds
2 cloves garlic, crushed
1 tbsp ghee
oil for frying

Method:

- Mix the gram flour and wholemeal flour together with 1 tbsp ghee.
- Add methi and coriander leaves with chopped potato and all the above ingredients.
- Add a little water to make a thick batter.
- Drop small amounts of the batter and deep fry in oil on a low temperature.
- Serve hot with chutney.

Medu Vada

Ingredients:

1 bowl urad dal
3 green chillies chopped
5 curry leaves chopped
1 cup coriander leaves chopped
½ cup grated coconut
¼ tsp black pepper
½ tsp salt according to taste
oil for frying

Method:

- Wash and soak urad dal for 3 hours.
- Liquidize coarsely to produce a thick batter.
- Add all the ingredients mentioned.
- With a wet hand, take a tbsp of paste, place on the hand and flatten.
- Make a hole in the middle with your thumb and deep fry till golden.
- This south Indian dish tastes nice with sambhar or coconut chutney.

Potato Vada

Ingredients:

1 lb potatoes
250 gms gram flour
5 green chillies crushed
1" piece of ginger
crushed 1 cup fresh
coriander chopped
1 tbsp sesame seeds
cooking oil
1 tsp cumin seeds
garam masala
1 chopped onion
1 tsp cumin powder
1¼ tsp salt

4 tsp sugar
Juice of 1 lemon
½ tsp cinnamon and
clove powder
pinch of asafoetida

Method:

- Boil potatoes, skin and mash.
- Add 1 tsp of salt, cumin powder, sugar, chillies, ginger, sesame seeds, coriander, lemon juice and mix well.
- In a separate pan heat two tablespoons of oil and fry the cumin seeds, asafoetida and onion; fry till onion becomes slightly brown in colour.
- Add the oil to the mashed potato and mix well.
- Mould mixture into small round balls.
- In a separate bowl sift gram flour and add ½ tsp of salt, slowly add water and stir continuously to make a thick batter.
- Add 1 tbsp oil to the batter.
- Roll potato balls in batter and deep fry till outer layer becomes golden brown.
- Serve hot with tomato chutney.

Vegetable Dahi Vada

Ingredients:

½ cup fresh peas
1 small piece of cabbage
4 potatoes
1 unripe banana
1 small carrot
4 green beans
few methi and spinach
leaves
pinch of sugar
1 lemon juice
1 tsp of salt
oil
5 curry leaves

1 bowl urad dal
8 green chillies crushed
2 florets of cauliflower
1" ginger paste
2 bowls yogurt
1 bowl coriander leaves
¼ tsp of salt
½ tsp of sugar

Method:

- Chop vegetables and boil with a pinch of salt.
- Soak urad dal for 3 hours and grind.
- Peel boiled potatoes and banana.
- Mix the boiled vegetables with the urad dal.
- Add salt, lemon juice, ginger, chillies and sugar.
- Make small balls and fry till they turn brown.
- Beat yogurt and salt and sugar to taste.
- Place the vada in a dish and spread the yogurt over the top.
- Garnish with coriander leaves.
- This tastes nice with sweet chutney.

Khaman Dhokra

Ingredients:

1lb chana dal (yellow
gram flour)
1 cup coriander leaves,
chopped
1 cup yogurt
few curry leaves
8 green chillies
½ cup grated coconut
1" ginger, crushed
2 big chillies, chopped
¾ cup of oil, to mix
mustard seeds
1 tsp sugar

asafoetida
1 ½ tsp eno
1 ½ tsp salt
½ tsp turmeric powder

Method:

• Soak chana dal for 5 hours.
• Drain all the water and mix in a blender (this should form a dry
  mixture).
• Mix this dal with yogurt, ginger, chillies, salt, sugar, turmeric
  powder and oil.
• If the mixture becomes too dry add 2 tbsp water.
• Using a steamer, grease a steel plate with oil.
• Add eno to the batter and fill a plate.
• Steam for ½ an hour.
• In a small pan heat a little oil. Once the oil is hot add mustard
  seeds, chopped chillies and curry leaves. Finally add a pinch of
  asafoetida.
• Pour the oil over the khaman dhokra and cut into square pieces.

Leela Marcha

Ingredients:

1 bowl peas
1 bowl moong dal
1" piece grated ginger
few crushed green chillies
½ cup chopped coriander leaves
1 tsp salt, ½ tsp turmeric powder,
garam masala, red chilli powder
1 lemon juice
3 tsp sugar and raisins
use the above masala (two pinches)
according to taste
2 cloves garlic crushed
¼ tsp of asafoetida
1 lb plain flour and
¼ tsp green food colouring
½ cup oil & 1 chopped onion
1stp fennel powder

Method:

- Soak moongdal for two hours.
- Boil potatoes and cut into small cubes.
- Grind peas coarsely.
- Heat oil and add moong dal.
- Stir and let it cook for few minutes.
- Once half cooked add peas, salt, and turmeric powder.
- Add ginger, chilli paste, red chilli powder and cook till done.
- Take the pan off the heat and add lemon, sugar, garam masala, fresh coriander, onion and fennel.
- Mix well.
- Mix the flour with oil, salt, a little food colour and water.
- Form a soft dough.
- Now roll a big roti from the flour and cut into four.
- Put the above filling in one of the segments and bring the sides together.
- Form a chilli shape.
- Deep fry until cooked throughly.
- Tastes very nice with sweet chutney.

Anghar

Ingredients:

Coconut masala:
1 fresh coconut grated
½ bowl cashew nuts crushed
3 crushed green chillies
½ lemon juice
2 tsp sugar
1 tsp salt
½ tsp cumin powder
½ cup fresh coriander chopped

Potato masala:
2lb fresh pototoes
1 tsp salt
3 tsps sugar
½ lemon juice
3 green chillies crushed
1" ginger crushed
1 tsp cumin powder

Batter:
3 cups gram flour
½ tsp salt
pinch of baking powder
1 tbsp hot oil

Method:

- Put all the ingredients and coconut in a bowl and mix throughly. Make small balls out of it and keep aside.
- Then boil potatoes, remove skin and mash. Add ingredients for potato masala. Take some mash in hand and flatten. Then put one ball of coconut masala and cover properly. Likewise make all the balls in the same way. Mix all ingredients for the batter and mix well with water.
- In a frying pan heat oil, dip the balls one at a time in the batter and deep fry till golden in colour, then remove and place on a kitchen towel.
- Now take fresh yogurt, whisk and add a pinch of salt, red chilli powder and mix well. In a long tray first layer the yougurt.
- Now on the halves put some green chutney then tamarind-date chutney then top it up with thin sev and fresh chopped coriander. Serve with yougurt.

Aloo Tiki

Ingredients:

1lb potatoes
1 carrot grated
½ cup green peas
1 small onion
4/5 crushed green chillies
1" grated ginger
2 tbsp cornflour or
(3 slices of bread)
2 tbsp oil
1 tsp cumin
pinch of asafoetida
½ a cup chopped

coriander leaves
½ tsp cumin powder
¼ tsp black pepper
1 tsp salt

Method:

• Boil potatoes and mash.
• Grate carrot.
• Coarsely grind peas or if frozen crush them.
• In a pan heat a little oil and temper with cumin and asafoetida.
• Add carrot,and peas and cook with ½ tsp salt, then add crushed chillies and ginger.
• Let it cool.
• Add 1 tbsp cornflour and ½ tsp salt, chopped coriander, and peas masala to the mashed potato.
• Roll to the size of walnut and press down to form shape.
• Coat all the tikis with cornflour.
• Fry golden brown and serve with sweet tamarind chutney.

Patra Leaves

Ingredients:

1 lb patra leaves
3 lb gram flour
1 tbsp wheat flour
7 cloves crushed garlic
2" crushed ginger
6 crushed green chillies
1 pkt tamarind
1 cup chopped coriander leaves.
1 tbsp red chilli powder
3 tbsp salt (according to taste)
14 tbsp sugar or jaggery
1 tsp turmeric powder
2 tbsp cumin and coriander powder
1 cup oil, ½ tsp asafoetida
1 cup yogurt

Method:

- Wash and remove the vein from the patra leaves.
- Roll each leaf with the rolling pin to crush all the veins.
- Mix the rest of the ingredients to form a thick batter.
- On a board put a leaf upside down and apply the batter evenly.
- On top of the first leaf put another leaf and apply batter.
- Likewise apply batter to three to four leaves and fold from the side.
- Now make roll and prepare all the patras.
- You may freeze the patras before steaming.
- In a pan put water and steam patras for at least one hour and let it cool down.
- Slice into round shapes.
- In a pan heat oil and temper sliced onion (optional) with mustard, cumin seeds,
  asafoetida and sesame seeds.
- Add patras and cook until slightly brown.
- You may sprinkle desiccated coconut and chopped coriander leaves.
- You may deep fry patras.

Bhel

Ingredients:

½ lb potatoes
½ lb puffed rice (mamra)
1 cup kala chana – soaked
1 cup wholemeal flour
½ tsp salt
1 cup fresh coriander
2 tbsp oil
1 onion finely chopped
1 raw mango finely chopped
1 cup sprouted moong
1 cup sev (made from gram flour)
date and tamarind (runny)
green chutney (runny)
garlic chutney (runny)

Method:

- Boil the potatoes, skin and cut into cubes.
- Wash the soaked chana and boil soft.
- Mix oil with the flour and make hard dough with a little water.
- Roll small puris, prick and deep fry.
- When cooled break into pieces, store in a container.
- When serving mix potatoes, channa, mamra, onions, moong and raw mango
- Add ½ tsp salt and red chilli powder.
- Mix the puri pieces with sev, then top it up with the three above-mentioned chutneys.
- To make chutney see page 4.

Spring Rolls

Ingredients:

4 onions cut length ways
2 pkts of beansprouts
3 potatoes grated
I small cabbage, chopped long
I cup coriander leaves
I tsp cumin seeds
4 carrots, grated
I tbsp cumin powder
Pinch of asafoetida/hing
8 green chillies, crushed
I ½" pieces ginger, crushed

I tbsp red chilli powder
½ tsp citric acid powder
3 tsp salt
7 tsp sugar
½ small bottle soya sauce
I tbsp cumin
2 pkts spring roll pastry

Method:

- Heat oil, add cumin seeds and asafoetida.
- Add onion and cook till light brown.
- Add cabbage, carrots, potatoes, chillies, ginger and salt.
- Toss for 5-6 minutes.
- Add beansprouts and soya sauce.
- Mix well and leave to cook.
- Remove from heat and drain away all liquid.
- Add sugar, cumin powder, citric acid and red chillies.
- Leave to cool.
- Add a little water to plain flour to make a paste.
- Take one layer of pastry and add filling.
- Cover all sides and roll, sealing the edges with paste.
- Deep fry rolls till golden.
- You may freeze and fry when required.

Vegetable Cutlets

Ingredients:

2 lb potatoes
small onion grated
½ cup peas, ½ cup corn
1 carrot
few green beans
½ cup crushed peanuts
1" crushed ginger
8 green chillies crushed
1 raw mango grated
½ cup chopped coriander
½ lemon juice
2 tbsp bread crumbs
2 tsp salt and little plain flour

Method:

- Cut carrot and green beans into small pieces.
- Now steam carrot, beans, peas and corn with a little salt.
- Boil potatoes.
- Mash potatoes and add all the above ingredients except plain flour and breadcrumbs.
- Mix well and make square cutlets or whatever shape you desire.
- Roll into the fine semonila.
- Shallow fry.
- Serve hot with your choice of chutney.

Uttapam

Ingredients:

3 bowls of rice
½ bowl urad dal
chopped green chillies
3 tomatoes finely chopped
2 onions finely chopped
chopped coriander leaves
2 tbsp cashew nuts
½ capsicum (red pepper)
1 tsp salt

Method:

- Soak rice and urad dal separately for 8 hours.
- Drain and liquidize separately adding some water.
- Mix together, add salt and keep aside for another 8 hours.
- Heat tawa and grease it.
- Now spread the batter evenly on the tawa and spread the chopped ingredients over it.
- Cover the pan and let it cook at low temperature.
- You may add all the chopped ingredients to the batter and then make uttapam.
- Once cooked on one side turn and cook on the other side.
- Eat with coconut chutney.

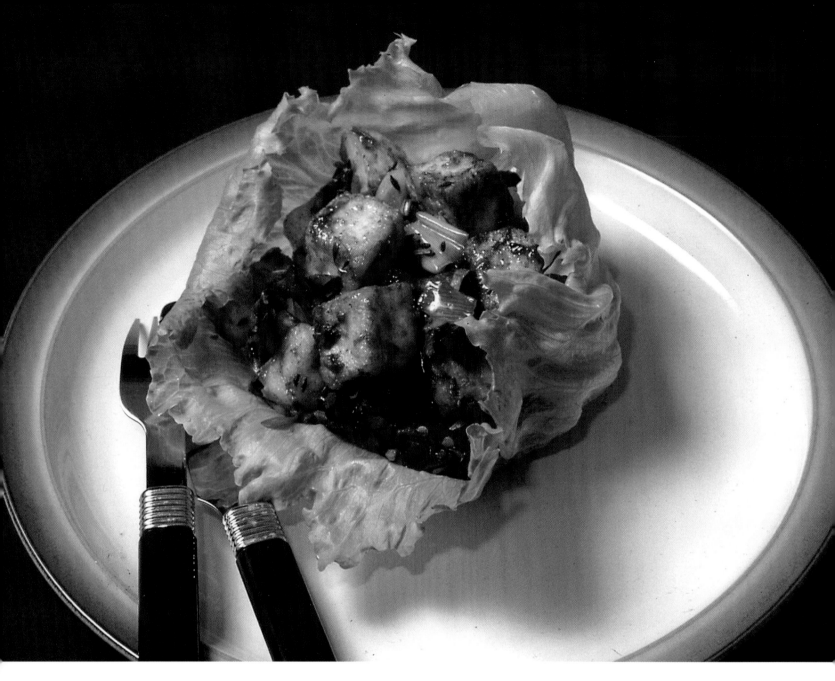

Chilli Paneer

Ingredients:

6 pints of milk
3 bunches of spring
onion cut into long strips
1 red hot chilli sliced
1 red capsicum sliced
4 cloves garlic crushed
1" ginger crushed
2 fresh green chillies
crushed
1 tsp cumin
1 tsp citric acid or lemon
juice

1 cup chopped coriander
leaves
1 tsp soya sauce
2 tsp oil
3 lettuce leaves
½ tsp red chilli powder
1 tsp salt
oil

Method:

- Boil milk and add lemon juice or citric acid to curdle the milk.
- Set aside to cool.
- Strain milk through a muslin cloth.
- Squeeze out all the whey and wash paneer throughly in cold water.
- Press paneer under a heavy weight for 2 hours (alternativley, you can buy the paneer ready made).
- Cut into rectangular pieces and fry until golden.
- Heat oil in a wok; add cumin, spring onions, red hot chillies, garlic and fresh ginger.
- Add salt.
- Toss and leave half cooked; now add capsicum, paneer, soya sauce, and red chillies and garnish with coriander leaves.

Bhagat Muthia

Ingredients:

1 bowl gram chana dal
2 chopped onions
5 tomatoes grated
½ tsp garam masala
1 tbsp dhanajiru
1 tbsp tomato paste
1 tsp mustard seed/rai
½ tsp cumin seeds.
pinch of asafoetida/hing
7 green chillies crushed
4 cloves garlic crushed
1" ginger crushed
1½ tsp salt

½ cup oil for seasoning
1 cup green coriander chopped
1tsp turmeric powder

Method:

• Soak chana dal for 4 hours.
• Wash and drain all the water.
• Now liquidize.
• Make sure there is no water left.
• Add ½ the above spices and shape them into round balls.
• Deep fry till golden brown.
• Heat 2 tbsp mustard & cumin seeds and a pinch of asafoetida.
• Add onion, fry till light pink.
• Now add the remaining crushed spices.
• Add chopped tomatoes.

• Stir well.
• Mix well and let it cook at a low temperature for 5 mins.
• Add all the fried balls.
• Add 1½ cups boiling water.
• Let it boil at low temperature till gravy becomes thick.
• Now add garam masala and garnish with coriander leaves.
• Tastes nice with nan, chapattis or parathas.

Stuffed Potato with Sweet Chutney

Ingredients:

2lb small potatoes
½ cup chana dal
2 pkts dates
1 pkt tamarind
2 tsp red chilli powder
1 small onion
5 cloves garlic crushed
1 cup coriander chopped
2 tsp salt
oil for frying
1 tsp cumin powder
½ tsp turmeric powder

Method:

• Soak chana dal in water overnight and then strain the dal.
• Heat oil and fry ½ cup chana dal till crispy.
• Add salt, turmeric powder and red chilli powder and mix well.
• Boil potatoes and peel skin.
• When partly hot make four cuts, keeping potato whole.
• Mix garlic, red chilli powder, salt, half the coriander leaves, 1 tsp oil, and cumin powder.
• Stuff this mixture into the potatoes.
• Boil the tamarind and dates in water and sieve the pulp.
• Add finely chopped onion, salt, red chilli powder, cumin powder and the rest of the coriander leaves and mix well to produce the sweet chutney.
• Keep four filled potatoes on the plate and spread sweet chutney over it.
• Sprinkle fried chana dal over it.

Crispy Bhajia (Maru Bhajia)

Ingredients:

2 lbs potatoes
250gm gram flour
50gm thick semolina or rice flour
1 small onion grated
1 cup fresh coriander chopped
½ cup fresh methi leaves chopped
oil to deep fry
2 tsp salt
4 cloves garlic minced
2 fresh green chilli chopped
1" piece ginger crushed
1 tbsp red chillie powder
1 tsp cumin powder
1 tsp sugar

Method:

- Peel and thinly slice potatoes, wash and soak in salted water (for 30 mins) drain water.
- To the gram flour, add onion, coriander and methi and mix well.
- Add salt, garlic, green chillies, chilli powder, ginger, cumin powder and sugar and mix into a thick batter using water.
- To the potatoes add the above ingredients and mix properly.
- Take some slices on a plate and sprinkle on the semolina or rice flour mix and deep fry in hot oil.
- Serve with maru bhajia chutney.

Chandu Bhajia

Ingredients:

1½ lb potatoes
2 tsp salt
1 bowl wheat flour
1 tsp red chilli powder
3 crushed green chillies
1 tbsp cumin powder
1" crushed ginger
½ cup chopped coriander leaves
4 cloves crushed garlic
oil for frying

Method:

- Wash potatoes and cut into very small cubes.
- To this add all the above ingredients and mix well.
- Add a little water if required.
- Add 1 tbsp of hot oil and mix well. They fry in hot oil until well cooked.
- Serve with sweet chutney.

Farari Pizza

Ingredients:

1 lb rajgira flour
250gms tomatoes grated
2 capsicums cut into small pieces
4 tbsp tomato ketchup
½ tsp salt and cumin
grated cheese
2 tbsp oil
250gms potatoes (½ tsp salt)
2 tbsp sesame seeds
3 green chillies finely chopped
1 tsp sugar
½ tsp of black pepper

Method:

- Add oil and a little salt to the rajgira flour and knead with water to make a soft dough.
- Use the dough to roll a base for the pizza and cook both sides on a skillet (frying pan).
- Heat oil, add cumin and tomatoes.
- Add salt, sugar and chilli and cook till the water evaporates.
- Remove skin from the potatoes and chop into small cubes.
- In a pan, heat some more oil, add cumin and sesame seeds and toast lightly.
- Now add potato cubes and cook on a low heat.
- Once almost cooked add chillies and salt.
- Now spread tomato mixture on top of the pizza base.
- Spread potato and capsicum and, on top, spread ketchup, green chillies and cheese.
- Bake in the oven for 20 mins.

Chilli Baigan

Ingredients:

1 big aubergine
1 bunch of spring onions
1 red and green capsicum
½ cup gram flour
oil for frying
5 cloves crushed garlic
½ tsp green chillies crushed
½ tsp salt
1 cup chopped coriander

Method:

• Cut aubergine into four and then cut thinly lengthwise.
• Sprinkle 1 tsp salt on to the aubergines.
• Leave to stand for 10 minutes.
• Sprinkle gram flour on the sliced aubergines.
• Deep fry aubergines, until crunchy.
• Cut spring onion and capsicum lengthwise.
• In a frying pan put 2 tbsp oil and add spring onion, garlic and green chilli.
• Stir a couple of times. Add capsicum and salt.
• Now mix everything together.
• Remove from the heat and garnish with coriander leaves.

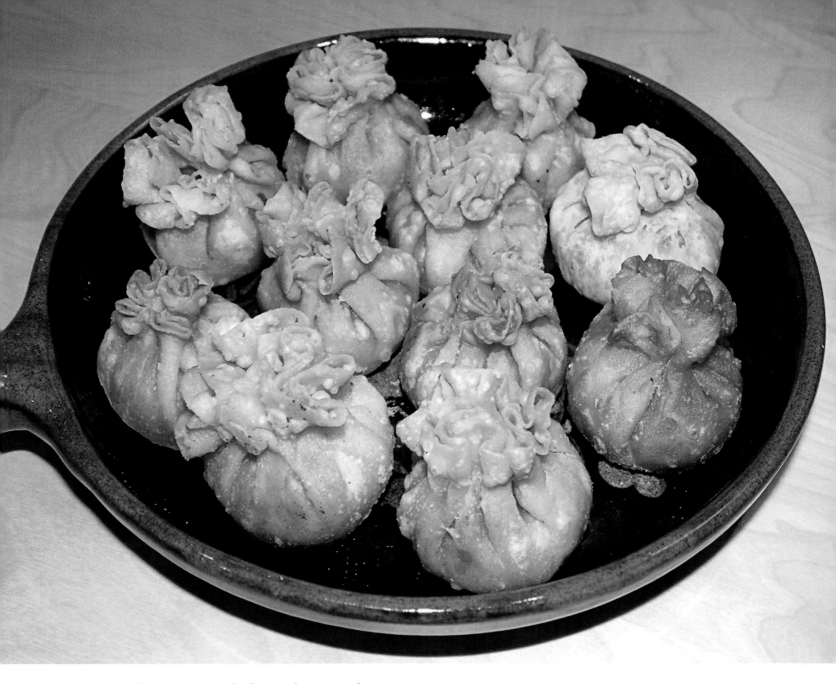

Peas Potly Kachori

Ingredients for peas masala:

2lb peas crushed
1 tbsp salt
4 tsp sugar
2" crushed ginger
3 cloves of crushed garlic
10 green chillies crushed
1 cup coriander leaves
¼ tsp cloves and cinnamon powder
1 lemon juice
1 cup oil
1 tsp cumin and 2 pinches of asafoetida
1 tbsp fennel powder

For the pastry:

1 lb plain flour
½ cup fine semolina
1 tsp salt
¾ cup oil
warm water
oil for frying

Method:

- Heat oil and temper with cumin and asafoetida.
- Add crushed peas with chillies, ginger, garlic and salt.
- Once cooked, add lemon juice, sugar, clove, cinnamon powder and fennel powder.
- Add chopped coriander leaves and form small balls.
- Add oil in the flour with salt, semolina and knead with the warm water to form a soft dough.
- Take a little dough and roll small puri so that it is thicker in the middle than the edges.
- Put a ball of the pea mixture in the middle and bring all the ends together in the centre.
- Give a twist to the gathered ends so that it should look like a blooming flower.
- Now fry all the kachories and eat with sweet or green chutney.

Makai Bhajia – Corn Pakoda

Ingredients:

3 corn on the cob
1 bowl gram flour
½ cup semolina
1 tsp salt, 1 tsp sugar
pinch of asafoetida/hing
1 cup green coriander leaves
oil
1" grated ginger
4 green chillies chopped
¼ tsp eno
1 tsp cumin powder
1 tbsp sesame seeds
Juice of half a lemon

Method:

• Roast the semolina dry in a pan.
• Grate the corn from the cob.
• Add all the rest of the ingredients to the corn and mix in a bowl.
• Add semolina and gram flour.
• Mix well and leave for 30 minutes.
• Drop small spoonfuls of the mixture in the hot oil and deep fry until golden brown.
• Eat with any chutney or tomato ketchup.

Farsi Puri

Ingredients:

3lb plain flour
1½ pkts butter (1/12 lb)
2 tsp salt
2 tsp coarse black
pepper powder
2 tsp coarse cumin
powder
2 tbsp sesame seeds

white in colour:

1 cup gram flour
½ a cup semolina
¼ tsp asafoetida
warm water
oil for frying

yellow in colour:

2 tsp crushed chillies
2 tsp ajwain
2 tbsp sesame

Method:

- In a pan add all the three flours.
- Add butter and mix well.
- Add the above masala and with warm water to form a firm dough.
- If you prefer a yellow colour puris, add the third part as well.
- Make small puri and prick with a fork.
- Let all the puris dry for 30 minutes.
- Now fry at medium temperature till light pink.
- Store in an airtight container and eat within 2 months.

Samosa

Ingredients for stuffing:

3 lbs peas
5 large potatoes
1 lb carrots
1 bowl chana dal
5 large onions, chopped
2 extra onions, chopped
2 bunches of coriander, chopped
2 tsp cumin powder
¾ tsp asafoetida
10 green chillies crushed
2 pieces ginger crushed
10 tsp sugar
3 tsp salt
3 tsp cumin powder
1 ½ tsp red chilli powder

1 ½ tsp garam masala
1 tsp citric acid
oil

Ingredients for pastry:

1 lb plain flour
½ tsp citric acid
½ cup oil
1 tsp salt
oil for brushing and frying
warm water

Method: (pastry preparation on page 6)

- Boil chana dal (gram dal) with a little salt.
- Strain dal.
- Cut potatoes, carrots and onions into small cubes. (Keep 2 chopped onions to one side.)
- Heat oil in a pan and fry cumin seeds, add asafoetida and chopped onions and cook until brown.
- Fry potatoes and carrots, boil peas (adding a little salt if peas are fresh) and then drain the water.
- Mix the fried onions, peas, chillies, ginger, salt, cumin powder, potatoes, carrots and boiled chana dal.
- Remove from heat. When the mixture has cooled add sugar, citric acid, red chilli powder, garam masala, coriander and the two chopped onions and mix well.

Moga Na Farari Vada

Method:

1 lb mogo casava
½ cup sago powder (saboodana flour)
1" crushed ginger
8 green chillies crushed
1 small potato
Juice of one lemon
1 tbsp cumin powder
½ cup chopped coriander leaves
½ tsp ground black pepper
3 tsp sugar and salt according to taste

Method:

• Boil mogo and potato.
• Mash both.
• While it is hot add all the above ingredients and form small balls like jambu.
• Heat oil and deep fry at medium temperature.
• All the vadas will puff up.
• Deep fry until golden.
• Serve hot with farazi chutney.

Suva Na Muthia

Ingredients:

1 bunch suva bhajia (dill)
½ tsp turmeric powder
1 grated onion
½ cup oil
1 bowl gram flour
8 green chillies crushed
½ cup rice flour
1" ginger crushed
1 bowl cooked rice
6 cloves garlic crushed
1 tsp sugar
½ cup coriander leaves
2 tsp salt

1 cup oil for tempering
1 tbsp cumin and
coriander powder
1 tsp cumin seeds and
sesame seeds
2 pinches of asafoetida

Method:

- Chop suva and wash.
- In a big bowl put all the above ingredients except for the cumin and sesame seeds and asafoetida ingredients.
- Mix well and form walnut size balls.
- Heat the oil and add the cumin seeds and asafoetida for tempering, then add sesame seeds to form a single layer.
- Now arrange muthias in the tempered oil.
- Do not put in all the muthias.
- Cook at low temperature till a light brown colour.
- Remove and repeat with the other balls.
- Once light brown colour add everything to the pan and cook at a low temperature for 45 minutes.

Onion Pancakes

Ingredients:

1lb gram flour
1 tbsp wheat flour
1 bunch of fenugreek
leaves
1 tbsp cumin powder
2 small onions chopped
1 tsp ajwain
2 cloves chopped garlic
1 tsp coriander and
cumin powder
4 green chillies chopped
1 tsp salt according to
taste

1" crushed ginger
½ tsp black pepper
1 tbsp yogurt
1 cup chopped coriander
leaves
oil
½ tsp sugar

Method:

- Add all the above ingredients to the gram flour and form a thick batter with warm water.
- Leave to stand for 2 hours, or you can make pancakes immediately.
- In a non-stick frying pan, add half a cup of the batter and spread to form a thin pancake.
- Apply tbsp oil round the pancake and once pink turn over to the other side, apply oil again.

Khamman Patra

Ingredients:

½ lb chana dal
2 tbsp peanuts
6 cloves garlic crushed
I bunch coriander leaves
I tsp fennel
½ tsp salt to taste
¼ tsp turmeric powder
½ tsp red chilli powder
½ cup desiccated coconut
6 green chillies chopped
I tbsp sesame seeds
I tbsp poppy seeds
I tsp sugar
I tbsp cumin
I tbsp coriander powder
garam masala
(if preferred)

Dough ingredients:

½ lb chapatti flour
½ lb gram flour
½ cup oil
½ tsp of salt

Method:

- Finely grind peanuts, desiccated coconut/green chilli, coriander leaves, cloves, salt, sugar, fennel, cumin and coriander in a food processor.
- Wash chana dal and drain all the water from it. Crush the dal.
- Steam until cooked, then let it cool.
- Now add salt, turmeric powder, crushed chilli, desiccated coconut, sesame seeds poppey and coriander leaves.
- To the gram flour and chapatti flour oil, salt, with the warm water and form a firm dough.
- Now roll a big chapatti from this dough.
- Spread the above crushed masala.
- On top of this, spread the chana dal masala.
- Now make a tight roll and cut into ½ " rounds.
- Press each round softly in your palm and roll in the plain flour.
- Now deep fry.
- Enjoy with any chutney.

Sev Khamni

Ingredients for Sev:

1 bowl gram flour
3 bowls butter milk
1½ tsp crushed green chillies
½ tsp turmeric powder
Salt according to taste

Ingredients for masala:

1 cup grated coconut
½ cup roasted peanut powder
3 tbs sesame seeds
4 green chillies finely chopped
few chopped coriander leaves
1 tbsp poppy seeds
ground sugar
salt and red chilli powder according to taste

Method:

• For sev mix add all the above sev ingredients and liquidize.
• Put the mixture on the heat in a pan and stir continuously at low temperature.
• Once it thickens put into the sev machine. (sev machines are available in most indian indgredient shops).
• Spread a little oil on the plate and with the machine make a small sev circle.
• Mix all the masala together and spread over the sev circle and cover with another sev circle.
• Again spread the masala and sprinkle with red chilli powder.
• Heat a little oil and add mustard seeds, sesame seeds, cumin and asafoetida/hing.
• Add green chillies and sprinkle on top of the dish.

Sweet Dishes

Amruti

Ingredients:

1 cup desiccated coconut
½ cup almond powder (coarse)
½ cup pistachio powder (coarse)
½ cup sugar
½ cup milk
½ tsp ghee
nutmeg and cardamom powder
2 whole cups milk powder
2 tsp self raising flour
1 ½ cup sugar syrup
decorate with either poppy seeds
or silver paper

Method:

- Add the coconut to the milk and leave for 2 hours.
- Now add ½ cup sugar and ghee and cook on a low heat.
- Once the milk part evaporates add almonds and pistachios.
- Add cardamom and nutmeg.
- Now add ½ tsp ghee and 2 tsp self raising flour to the milk powder and knead with the warm milk to form a soft smooth dough.
- Knead till dough becomes smooth.
- Take a small portion of the dough and flatten in the palm of your hand.
- Fill coconut in the middle of the milk powder puri and cover properly to form an oval shap.
- Leave to set.
- Repeat with the remaining mixture.
- Now fry in the oil.
- Make 1 ½ cups sugar syrup and once the amruti are cold add to the syrup.
- Leave to soak in the syrup for 2 hours then remove and set a side.
- Coat with the silver paper or poppy seeds.

Angoor Rabdi

Ingredients:

3 litres full cream milk
2 litres full cream milk
2 bowl sugar (1 ½ lb)
1 cup sugar
1 tsp citric powder
2 tbsp almond and
pistachio slices
few strands of saffron
¼ tsp cardamom
a pinch of nutmeg

Method:

- First boil 2 litres of milk with 2 tbsp water.
- Let it boil till thick and leave to cool.
- When milk is luke warm, add the sugar.
- Add cardamom and nutmeg.
- In another heavy based pan boil 3 litres of milk with 2 tbsp water.
- Curdle the milk by adding the citric powder.
- Strain all the water using a sieve, and wash in cold water and wrap in a tea towel.
- Squeeze any excess water by wrapping in a tea towel.
- Slightly knead the curd (paneer) and form small round balls. Set aside.
- In another pan boil 4 bowls of water with sugar
- Once the water starts to boil add this small round balls into it and let it boil for 5 minutes.
- Take the balls out from the syrup and set aside.
- Once cold add to the milk and refrigerate for 4 hours.
- Now add saffron, sliced almonds and pistachio and serve.

Semolina Ghughra

Ingredients:

500g plain flour
1 bowl fine semolina (250g)
1 bowl ghee (250gm)
1 ½ bowls sugar (500g)
1 bowl crushed almonds
1 bowl pistachios (crushed)
1 bowl desiccated coconut
1 tsp fennel seed powder
¼ tsp nutmeg
¼ tsp cardamom
few strands of saffron
¾ cups of milk
1 cup of ghee as required

Method:

• Roast semolina with ghee till golden brown.
• Add almonds, pistachios and coconut.
• Remove from the heat.
• Now add nutmeg, cardamom, fennel, saffron and sugar.
• Let it cool completely.
• Knead plain flour with ghee and warm milk.
• Make small round puri.
• Put a little filling in the middle.
• Make semicircles by bringing the sides together.
• With the help of your finger, make a twisting pattern on the circular edge.
• Prepare all ghughras and deep fry in the oil at a low temperature.
• Serve cold.

Blooming Flower

Ingredients:

1 bowl cashew nuts, ground finely
¼ cup almonds ground coarsely
½ cup pistachios ground coarsely
½ a bowl sugar
pinch of nutmeg
pinch of cardamom powder
1 tbsp coconut powder
2 pinches food red colouring
(according to your desire)

Method:

- Make sugar syrup, add sugar and ½ a cup water. (*Thread Consistency*)
- Add red colour to the syrup.
- Take enough syrup to mix with the almond and pistachio powder.
- Now add coconut powder and mix well to form small balls.
- In a separate bowl, mix the ground cashew nuts, nutmeg and form a dough.
- Take enough dough in the palm of your hand and spread to cover the almond and pistachio balls.
- Put the covered balls on the plastic sheet and, with a sharp knife, make six cuts on the top so that it looks like a blooming flower.
- Leave to cool for 1 hour before serving.

(*Thread Consistency*): The liquid sugar may be pulled into brittle threads between the fingers. Or, take a small amount of the syrup onto a spoon, and drop it from about 2-inches above the pan. Let it drip into the pan. If it spins a long thread, like a spider web, it's done.

Crunchy Chocolate Barfi

Ingredients:

½ bowl crushed ginger biscuits
1 bowl cornflakes (crushed)
1 bowl rice crisps (crushed)
1 bowl crushed almond
1 bowl crushed pistachio
1 bowl crushed cashew nuts
1½ bowls crushed digestive biscuits
50gm butter or margarine
2 tbsp cocoa powder
1 small tin golden syrup
2 large bars cooking chocolate

Method:

• Melt butter and add golden syrup, keep stirring all the time.
• Add cocoa powder.
• Now add the rest of the ingredients to the pan and mix thoroughly for 5 to 6 minutes.
• Continue cooking on a very low heat.
• Now spread the mixture in a lightley buttered and lined tray.
• Press firmly and evenly and leave to cool down completely.
• Melt chocolate slowly and spread evenly on the nut tray and tap the tray so that chocolate spreads smoothly and evenly.
• Once completely cool cut into pieces.
• Very popular with kids!

Thabdi – Milk Cake

Ingredients:

300 ml double cream
8 pints of milk for paneer
1 bowl milk powder (½ lb)
1 ½ bowls sugar
¼ tsp nutmeg powder
1 tsp citric acid powder
¼ tsp cardamom powder

Method:

- Heat the milk with ¼ cup of water until it boils.
- Now add citric powder to it to make paneer.
- Wash in cold water.
- Strain all the water from the paneer and wrap in the cloth.
- In another heavy-based pan boil double cream and sugar.
- Once it starts to boil, lower the heat and continue stirring.
- Once it becomes thick, add milk powder, paneer, nutmeg and cardamom powder.
- Mix well and place into a lightly buttered tray and form into a round shape.
- Leave to cool and turn the tray upside down on a flat surface.
- Serve as you wish.

Kaju Anjeer Patra

Ingredients:

1 lb ground cashew nuts
1pkt anjeer (figs)
pinch of nutmeg
1 bowl sugar
1 cup milk
silver paper foil
two plastic sheets

Method:

- Boil figs in the milk till quite thick.
- Make sugar syrup, add sugar and ½ a cup water; *(*for thread consistency - refer to page 71)*
- In a large bowl, mix enough of the sugar syrup with the ground cashew nuts to form a soft dough.
- Add nutmeg and mix well.
- On the plastic sheet, roll the dough into a big circle covering up with another plastic sheet to make it easy.
- Spread fig mixture evenly on the circle and softly roll with the help of plastic in the beginning; leaving the plastic continue rolling.
- Let it dry.
- Cut into ½" circle very softly with a very sharp knife.
- Decorate with silver paper, if you prefer.

Ice Halvo

Ingredients:

1 bowl plain flour
2 bowls sugar
1 bowl ghee
2 bowls water
sugar syrup, colours yellow or
pink (added in small amounts)
almonds and pistachio, cut
into slices
½ tsp cardamom
grease proof paper
plastic paper

Method:

- Mix 2 bowls of water to 1 bowl of plain flour and leave overnight.
- Next day make sugar syrup, using 2 bowls sugar and 2 bowls of water;
  (*for thread consistency - refer to page 71)
- Warm one tablespoon of ghee in a thick pan and pour the plain flour mixture in to it.
- Add half the sugar syrup to it, and stir constantly.
- As soon as it starts to thicken add a little sugar syrup at a time.
- Keep stirring all the time.
- When all the sugar syrup is used add a little ghee at a time.
- Keep on stirring all the time and use all the ghee.
- As soon as it becomes thick and white in colour, and leaves the pan, it is ready.
- This process will take about 2 hours.
- Put the mixture on greaseproof paper and roll with the rolling pin.
- Now sprinkle almonds, cardamom and pistachio and cover with the plastic paper.
- Again roll so that all the nuts are well settled and leave overnight to dry.
- Next day with the butter paper cut into 5" square pieces.

Chocolate Pista Barfi

Ingredients:

1 ½ lb milk powder
1 ½ bowls sugar
1 bowl coarse pistachio
½ tsp cardamom powder
½ cup cocoa powder
2 pinches of nutmeg powder
½ cup ghee
few slices of almond and pistachio
2 tbsp ghee

Method:

- In a pan make two strand of sugar syrup.
- Divide the syrup into three parts.
- Heat milk and ghee and once coming to boiling point add to the milk powder and mix well.
- Divide this powder into three parts.
- In the first syrup add one part of the powder with pistachio and ¼ tsp cardamom powder.
- Spread this thinly on the plastic sheet.
- Now warm the syrup again and add cocoa powder to the second part of the syrup.
- Add this to the second part of the milk powder and mix well.
- Now spread this evenly on the pistachio barfi.
- Warm the third part of the syrup and add the remaining milk powder with cardamom and nutmeg.
- Mix well and spread on top of the second layer evenly.
- Press smoothly and decorate with almond and pistachio slices.
- Once cool cut into pieces.

Bhangi Bundi Na Ladoo

Ingredients:

1lb gram flour
1½ bowls warm water
3 bowls sugar syrup
1 tbsp melted ghee
1 tsp mace powder
ghee for frying
½ tsp yellow food colouring
¼ tsp saffron
¼ tsp nutmeg
¼ tsp cardamom
few almonds and pistachios chopped

Method:

• Mix the gram flour with 1½ bowls of warm water to make a thick batter.
• Add 1 tbsp melted ghee and yellow food colouring.
• Heat ghee in a frying pan.
• Use a jara-type of big spoon with small holes in it.
• Hold this jara over the frying pan and put batter in it.
• Small bundies will start falling in the frying pan and when it comes up it's ready.
• Remove it with the help of the jara.
• Make two thread sugar syrup adding a little yellow food colouring.
• Grind all bundis in a chopper and mix with sugar syrup.
• Add almonds, pistachios, nutmeg and cardamom powder.
• When cold make small round balls - ladoos.

Dark Gulab Jambu with fresh cream

Ingredients:

500gm of mawa (milk powder)
1 lb sugar
¼ lb semolina
5 bowls water
oil for frying
1 cup milk
¼ tsp baking powder
few thin slices of almond
and pistachio
few strands of saffron
fresh double cream (small pot)

Method:

- Soak semolina in the milk for one hour
- Add ½ tsp of bicarbonate soda.
- Mix with mawa till it turns pink.
- Use the mixture to make round balls and leave aside to dry.
- Heat oil in a frying pan and fry balls on a low temperature.
- Make sugar syrup of one thread consistency and drop the gulab jambu in after they have cooled. *(*for thread consistency - refer to page 71)*
- Leave to stand overnight.
- Add sugar to the cream and mix well with a spoon.
- Make a slit on one side of jambu and fill with the cream.
- Garnish with pistachio and almond slices.
- Before serving cut into halves.

Cassava Biscuits (Mogo)

Ingredients:

1 ½ cups cassava flour
½ lb butter
1 bowl sugar
1 bowl desiccated coconut
½ bowl ground cashew nuts
5 tbsp milk
¼ tsp bicarbonate of soda
1 tsp milk
1 tsp cardamom and a few
strands
of saffron

Method:

- Add saffron to 1 tbsp of warm milk.
- Mix sugar and butter till creamy.
- Add bicarbonate of soda.
- Add cassava flour, saffron, ground cashew nuts, coconut and milk and mix well.
- Form into round balls.
- Arrange them in the tray and bake at gas mark 4-6.
- When cool, store in an airtight container.

Rasgulla

Ingredients:

4 pints of milk
½ tsp citric acid
2 bowls sugar
few cardamom seeds
5 bowls of water

Method:

- Boil milk and add citric acid to curdle the milk.
- Strain and leave to cool and wash paneer in cold water and leave it in the tea-towel.
- Squeeze out liquid and add cardamom seeds.
- Knead well and form round balls (walnut size).
- In a big pan boil water and sugar.
- While it is boiling add balls into it and cover the pan.
- Keep boiling at high temperature for 8 to 10 minutes.
- Turn once and lower the temperature.
- Keep boiling for 8 to 10 minutes.
- Make sure that the sugar syrup does not become thick.
- Leave to cool and serve.

Marble Barfi

Ingredients:

500 gms milk powder or mawa
1 cup milk
1 ½ tbsp ghee
½ lb sugar
1 bar white cooking chocolate
1 bar brown cooking chocolate
½ tsp nutmeg and cardamom powder

Method:

- In a saucepan make sugar syrup with 1 bowl of water.
- Warm milk and ghee and add to the milk powder to make a mixture.
- Add cardamom and nutmeg powder.
- When the sugar syrup becomes 2 thread consistency add the above milk powder. *(*for thread consistency - refer to page 71)*
- Mix well and spread in the tray lined with the plastic sheet or butter paper.
- Press evenly with a steel bowl.
- Now melt the brown chocolate.
- Spread on the barfi evenly.
- Now melt white chocolate and spread on the brown chocolate.
- With the spoon stir and spread in such a manner that a marble pattern forms. Once cool cut into square pieces.

Kataifi (Greek Dish)

Ingredients:

1 pkt of greek frozen vermicelli (leave
  to thaw for 1 hour)
1 bowl coarse ground almond powder
1 bowl ground pistachios (coarse)
1 bowl ground cashew nuts (coarse)
1 bowl ground sugar
½ pkt butter
1 tbsp cinnamon powder
1 tsp nutmeg powder
1 tsp cardamom powder
golden syrup or honey to brush up
flakes of almonds and pistachios

Method:

• Mix together almond, pistachio, cashew nuts, sugar, cinnamon,
  cardamom and nutmeg.
• Add melted butter and form oblong balls.
• Open the packet and slowly peel and cut 3" widths of vermicelli.
• Cover the oblong balls with it.
• Keep them on the baking tray and brush with melted butter.
• Bake them in the oven at gas mark 4 till they turn golden brown.
• Leave to cool.
• Heat syrup and honey and brush on the rolls.
• Sprinkle thin slices of almond and pistachio.

Tri-Rangi Sandesh

Ingredients:

2 cups of milk powder
1 cup ground pistachio powder (coarse)
2 tbsp ghee
1 tbsp icing sugar
1 tbsp milk
½ tsp nutmeg
2 tbsp of sliced pistachios
¼ tsp cinnamon powder
few strands of saffron
½ lb of sugar
2 tbsp desiccated coconut
¼ tsp red and yellow colouring

Method:

- Mix one cup of milk powder with 2 tbsp ghee, pistachios and icing sugar, then form small balls.
- In another pan mix the remaining milk powder, ghee and pistachio powder (khoya).
- Cook gently on low temperature.
- Remove from the heat and mix icing sugar, nutmeg, cardamom and saffron. Mix well and make small round balls.
- Make sugar syrup, divide into two parts.
- Add ½ tsp of ghee to the yellow part and the red part.
- Divide khoya to each colour so that you have red and yellow colour khoya.
- Take a small portion of the yellow colour khoya, and flatten in the palm of hand. Then cover the small rounds balls with the yellow khoya.
- Make sure it is smooth you can use little milk if required.
- Now flatten red colour khoya and cover yellow ball smoothly, use little milk if required to smooth over.
- Roll all balls in the desiccated coconut powder and serve sliced.

Plain Gulab Jambu

Ingredients:

1 bowl milk powder
1 tbsp plain four
1 tbsp self raising flour
2 tbsp melted ghee
1 ½ bowls sugar
a pinch of bicarbonate soda
few strands of saffron
2 pinches of nutmeg and cardamom
½ cup warm water
oil for frying

Method:

- Mix sugar with three cups of water and boil until it forms a syrup.
- In a pan mix milk powder, plain flour, self raising flour, cardamom, nutmeg, saffron and a pinch of bicarbonate soda.
- Using warm water make a soft dough, knead quickly.
- Separate into equally sized round balls and set aside for 30 mins.
- Heat oil in a frying pan and fry balls on a very low temperature.
- Turn gently and fry till brown.
- Remove from oil and allow to cool.
- Once cooled dip the jambus in the syrup.
- After four hours place jambus in a separate container.
- Before serving heat the syrup a little.
- Serve warm.

Adadiya

Ingredients:

1 bowl adadiya flour
1 tbsp ghee
3 tbsp milk
1 ½ cups ground almonds
1 cup ground pistachio
¼ cup gum arabic
2 cups sugar
1 tsp ground mace
1 tsp cardamom
1 tsp nutmeg
few strands of saffron
2 bowls of ghee

Method:

• Boil 1 tbsp ghee and 3 tbsp milk then add to flour for mixture (dhrabo).
• Keep for 10 mins then sift in a sieve.
• Roast flour with two cups of ghee till the flour becomes golden brown.
• Add gum arabic little by little till the mixture puffs up.
• Remove form the heat and add almonds, pistachio, saffron cardamom and nutmeg.
• Make a sugar the syrup to a thick consistency.
• Add syrup to the roasted flour and mix well.
• Mould into balls whilst warm or spread evenly in a tray.

Pistachio Barfi

Ingredients:

1 lb coarsely ground pistachios
2 bowls of sugar (1lb)
2 tbsp ghee
125mg double cream
¼ tsp nutmeg and cardamom powder
1 lb milk powder
1 pt milk
½ cup milk
2 pinches of green food colouring

Method:

- Heat one pint of milk, mix in sugar and reduce until about one cup is left.
- Add a few drops of green colour to syrup.
- Keep aside one cup of ground (coarse) pistachio.
- Mix two tbsp of ghee with ½ cup of milk, heat and add this to the milk powder.
- Add the ground pistachios, cream and milk syrup to the mixture of milk powder and mix well.
- Add nutmeg and cardamom powder.
- Lay greaseproof paper on a plate and spread the mixture, press evenly with the base of a flat bowl.
- Sprinkle pistachios evenly on top and again press with a flat bowl.
- When cool cut into square pieces.

Habsi Halvo (In the Microwave)

Ingredients:

3 bowls milk powder
3 bowls almond pieces
2½ bowls pistachio pieces
1 ½ bowls cashew nut pieces
2 bowls brown sugar
500ml double cream
1 cup milk
½ tsp cardamom
½ tsp nutmeg
½ tsp saffron
½ cup cashew nuts and pistachio
cardamom and saffron to decorate

Method:

- In a big glass bowl add all the above ingredients.
- Mix well and put in the microwave for two minutes
- Stir twice and repeat the process for 10 mins altogether, stirring every 2 mins.
- Once the ghee separates from the halvo and the colour becomes brown it is ready.
- If the colour is not brown add a little milk and put in the microwave for two minutes.
- Now add saffron, nutmeg and cardamom.
- Keep on stirring till all the ghee is soaked.
- In a tray put a plastic sheet and spread the halvo.
- Decorate with cashew nuts, pistachios, cardamon and saffron.
- Cut into square pieces.

Anjeer Halvo

Ingredients:

¼ lb anjeer (dry figs)
250 gm milk powder
1 tbsp ghee
½ cup milk
½ cup cashew nut pieces
¾ cup sugar
1 tbsp ghee
¼ tsp nutmeg powder
1 tbsp rose essence if preferred
2 tbsp ginger powder
almonds and pistachio slices

Method:

- Wash figs, wipe them and chop into small pieces.
- Soak the figs in water for 4 hours.
- Now boil figs.
- Add one tbsp ghee and cashew nuts.
- Boil for 15 minutes.
- Add sugar and cook until the figs form a thick syrup and add the nutmeg.
- Mix milk powder with ghee and milk and mix gently.
- Add this to the fig mixture, mix well.
- Spread the mixture in a greaseproof lined tray.
- Decorate with almond and pistachio pieces and cut into squares.
- Use the same method to make dry fruit halvo with cashew nuts.
- Almonds and pistachio.
- Soak this for one hour and follow the above method.

Ayurvedic Shahi Gundar Halvasan

Ingredients:

1 lb coarse wheat flour
1 bowl ghee
½ lb ginger juice
¾ lb Jaggery
1 bowl milk
½ bowl cashew nuts coarsely ground
1 cup black gum arabic
1 tsp black pepper
cardamom, saffron & nutmeg
almonds and pistachio slices
½ bowl magajtari seeds

(can buy from the Indian shops)
½ bowl coarse ground almonds
½ cup dry black grapes
½ cup pistachios coarsely ground
few dry apricots, dry figs, walnuts coarsely ground (to fill one cup)
1 tbsp fenugreek powder
2 tbsp fennel powder

Method:

- In a big pan roast wheat flour with ghee.
- Once it starts becoming pink add the edible gum in small amounts.
- Take it off the heat and add almond, pistachio, cashew nuts, walnuts and magajtari.
- In another pan boil milk.
- Add chopped apricots and figs.
- Once the milk thickens add roasted flour, jaggery, ginger juice, fennel, fenugreek powder, pepper, nutmeg, cardamom and saffron.
- Mix well.
- Roll into small balls. Flatten from the top.
- Decorate each ball with almonds and pistachio slices.

Rasmalai

Ingredients:

8 pints of milk
1 tbsp citric acid
3 bowls sugar
5 bowls water
2 pinches of nutmeg, cardamom and saffron
4 pints milk
¾ bowl sugar
few slices almonds and pistachios

Method:

- Boil 4 pints of milk and reduce until 2 pints remain.
- Remove from heat, let it cool then add sugar and evaporated milk.
- Add nutmeg and cardamom.
- Heat 8 pints of milk once it starts to boil add citric acid, the milk will curdle.
- Remove from heat and strain away excess liquid, leaving it to curd (This is paneer).
- Rinse paneer in cold water.
- Spread paneer on a dry cloth and drain all liquid. Knead paneer in the cloth.
- Divide paneer into equal balls.
- In another pan place two bowls of sugar in 5 bowls of water and boil.
- Drop paneer balls in and allow to boil.
- After 20 minutes remove balls from sugar water and dip in milk.
- Arrange rasmalai on the plate.
- Garnish with almonds, pistachios and saffron.

Semolina Siro with Pineapple

Ingredients:

1 bowl semolina
1 bowl pineapple
1 pint milk and water
mixed
½ bowl sugar
1 pkt butter
¼ tsp nutmeg and
cardamom powder
few strands of saffron
2 tbsp slices of almond
and pistachios

Method:

• Cut pineapple into small pieces.
• In a pan roast semolina with butter and ghee till dark pink.
• Boil the milk and water mixture.
• Once the semolina is roasted add milk.
• As soon as the milk is absorbed add sugar and pineapple.
• Mix well and decorate with almond and pistachio slices.

Jalebi

Ingredients:

3 cups of plain flour
1 tbsp yogurt
3 cups sugar syrup
1 tbsp gram flour
oil to fry
few strands of saffron
2 pinches yellow food colouring
1 pinch cardamon powder
sliced almonds and pistachios for
decoration

Method:

- Mix 1 ½ tbsp yogurt and half cup plain flour.
- Make a thick batter by adding the required amount of water.
- Leave batter to stand for one day, allowing it to ferment.
- After one day add to the batter, gram flour and plain flour and colour.
- Add water to make a thick batter.
- Leave to stand over night.
- Make sugar syrup with one thread consistency. *(*for thread consistency - refer to page 71)*
- Add saffron to the syrup.
- Heat oil in a frying pan.
- Use either a funnel or piping bag and fill with the batter.
- Make circular jalebi directly into the oil.
- Fry both sides and dip in the syrup.
- Place jalebi up-right in a plate allowing excess syrup to run down.
- Decorate with saffron, cardamom power, almonds and pistachios.

Sonpapdi

Ingredients:

½ kg gram flour
½ kg ghee
¼ kg sugar
½ lemon juice
few almonds and pistachio slices
½ tsp cardamom powder
few strands of saffron

Method:

- In a heavy pan roast flour with ghee.
- Once the aroma of the flour comes remove from the heat. Add saffron.
- Make sure the flour remains warm all the time.
- In another pan make a strong sugar syrup. Do not stir the syrup.
- Check the syrup by dipping in the tip of a match stick.
- Remove and drop syrup on to the work top. If it becomes hard the syrup is ready.
- Once the syrup is ready add lemon juice and spread in the tray.
- When the syrup becomes cold add the warm flour.
- With the help of two flat spoons (spatula) start bringing the flour from the two ends together. A thread of the syrup will form.
- When all the flour is mixed with the syrup, quickly roll on a hard surface and spread the almond, pistachio and cardamom powder on it.

Chocolate Balls

Ingredients:

12 digestive biscuits
6 tbsp drinking chocolate
3oz margarine
5 tbsp desiccated coconut
1 small tin condensed milk
for coating chocolate chips
2 tbsp desiccated coconut

Method:

- Crush biscuits.
- Add chocolate powder and coconut.
- Melt margarine and add to the above mixture.
- Add condensed milk and mix well.
- Make 14 balls.
- Coat 7 balls in desiccated coconut and another 7 balls in chocolate chips.

Laapsi (A delicious dessert from course wheat)

Ingredients:

1 bowl broken wheat (course)
¾ bowl sugar or jaggery
1 bowl ghee
1 tbsp cardamom powder
1 tbsp nutmeg powder
few strands of saffron
few raisins
thin slices of almonds and pistachios
few fennel seeds

Method:

- Heat ghee in a pan and fry wheat stirring continuously till it turns golden brown.
- Boil four cups of water in a separate pan.
- Add the water to the cooked wheat, stirring occasionally till the water begins to boil.
- Reduce the heat and cook, stirring frequently till the wheat is cooked.
- Add sugar and cardamom powder.
- Mix well.
- Cook on a low temperature till ghee separates.
- Add all the above ingredients and allow the laapsi to cool.
- Serve hot.

Basoondi with Puri

Ingredients:

6 pints of milk
2 pinches nutmeg powder
2 pinches cardamom
powder
2 tbsp almond slices
1 pinch mace powder
1 tbsp pistachio slices
½ a cup sugar
few strands of saffron
few charodi (type of nuts)

Puri:

1 bowl wholemeal flour
2 tbsp oil
½ cup cold milk
little hot water
oil for frying

Method:

- In a pan add ¼ cup water and add milk to boil.
- Once it starts to boil transfer into another pan and boil again.
- Now boil at medium gas and keep stirring all the time, reduce until you are left with 2 cups.
- Now add all the above ingredients.
- Allow to cool.

Method:

- In a bowl take wheatflour.
- Add 2 tbsp oil.
- Mix well and knead dough with the milk and a little hot water.
- Dough should be a little harder than chapatti flour.
- Roll small puri and deep fry in the oil.

Cassatta Barfi

Ingredients:

1 kg milk powder
1 cup milk
3 tbsp ghee
2 bowls sugar (500gm)
3 tbsp cocoa powder
2 pinches green colouring
3 pinches yellow colouring
4 drops vanilla essence
½ tsp cardamom powder

Method:

- Make a thick sugar syrup with 2 bowls sugar and 2 bowls water.
- Just before the syrup is ready, mix ghee and milk into the milk powder.
- Divide syrup into three parts.
- Add colours to each parts.
- Put vanilla essence in the yellow colour and in another the cardamom powder, with the green colour and cocoa powder in the third.
- Divide milk powder into three parts.
- Mix each part into the above different syrups.
- If the syrup has become cold warm it up.
- In a greaseproof lined tray spread the green barfi, then the yellow barfi and finally the brown chocolate barfi.

Mango Pulp Pudding

Ingredients:

1 tin mango pulp or fresh pulp
½ cup urad dal
1 cup rice
few sliced pistachios
few sliced cashew nuts

Method:

• Soak the urad dal and rice in water, separately overnight.
• Next morning wash and blend in a liquidizer separately, then mix.
• Keep aside to ferment for at least seven hours.
• Use the mixture to make pancakes and cut into small pieces.
• Dip pancake pieces in mango pulp.
• Garnish with sliced pistachios and cashew nuts.
• Serve cold.

Malindi Halvo

Ingredients:

500g whole wheat
½ cup varanga flour
½ potato powder
1 lb almond
¼ tsp yellow colour
pinch red colour
½ cup pistachio
500g sugar
250g ghee
1 tsp cardamom powder
few strands of saffron
½ lemon juice

Method:

- Wash and soak wheat overnight.
- Next day wash and soak again. On the third day liquidize. Squeeze out all the starch from the wheat.
- Now add a little water to the remaining liquidized wheat and liquidize again.
- Add this milky liquid to the above starch.
- Boil almonds and remove skins.
- Cut into two and keep aside.
- Do this one day ahead so that the almonds become dry. Cut pistachios into 2 parts.
- Now mix the starch, potato powder and varanga flour together. Mix well so that you do not see any lumps.
- In a big pan put 1 tbsp ghee and add the starch.
- Now make sugar syrup. Syrup to be a thick consistency. Add food colouring to the syrup.
- Now add ½ the syrup to the starch and stir at low temperature all the time.
- Keep the temperature low to prevent lumps. Keep adding 1 tbsp sugar syrup to the mixture while still stirring.
- Finish all the syrup and then start adding ghee to the mixture. This halva will take about 1½ hours to cook.
- When the ghee separates, the halva is cooked. Add the lemon juice.
- Garnish with almonds, pistachios and cardamom.
- Let it cool down. Now fill the plastic bag and make a thick roll.
- Put in the fridge and when ready to eat cut into pieces.
- Spread on to the tray and cut into square pieces.

Cashew nut and Pistacho Rolls

Ingredients

3 bowls fine cashew nuts powder
1 bowl each of ground almonds and pistachos
½ bowl sweet bundi (you can buy from the indian sweet shop)
2 bowls sugar and 1 bowl water (to make syrup).
¼ tsp nutmeg and cardamom
few strands of saffron
edible silver foil

Method:

- Crush bundi, add almonds, pistachos, saffron, cardamom and nutmeg.
- Now from the sugar syrup add ½ cup of syrup to the above mixture and form small rolls.
- Add the cashew nuts to the remaining syrup and form a soft dough.
- Roll this into a large thin roti on a plastic sheet.
- Put rolls on the top of roti and with the help of the plastic cover roll tight.
- A rolls are covered in the cashew nut roti and smoothed well.
- Finish all rolls accordingly.
- Now let it dry for three hours then cut each roll into 2 inch strips.
- Decorate with silver paper.

Almond Nut Sandwich

Ingredients:

1 ½ lbs desiccated coconut
250g almonds coarsly ground
250g pistachios coarsly ground
500g sugar
10 tbsp drinking chocolate
2 tbsp ghee (butter)
3 cups milk
1 tsp cardamom powder

Method:

• Boil milk and sugar to form a thick syrup.
• Divide syrup in two parts.
• Add one tablespoon ghee and the drinking chocolate to the almonds and pistachos.
• Add half the syrup to it and mix well.
• To the second half of the syrup, add coconut and one teaspoon of cardamom powder and one tablespoon ghee. Keep warm.
• Now in a big dish or tray put greaseproof paper and spread half the coconut mixture. Press and spread the almonds and pistacho mixture over it.
• Top up with coconut mixture. Thus making a sandwich. Let it cool.
• Cut into pieces.

Kamal Khaja

Ingredients for filling:

½ lb mawa (milkpower)
3/4 tbsp cream/malai
2 tbsp almonds coarsely ground
2 tbsp pistachios coarsely ground
2 tbsp cashew nuts coarsely ground
4 tbsp ground sugar

Ingredients for pastry:

1 ½ cup plain flour
1 pinch salt
3 tbsp plain flour
3 tbsp ghee for paste

Syrup:

2 cups water

Method:

- Mix mawa and malai and put on heat and keep stirring until the milk has evaporated. Remove from the heat and let it cool, then add sugar and all the nuts. Mix and make small balls.
- Add oil and salt the pastry flour, then knead into a soft, smooth dough. Make portions. Take one part and make 7 parts out of it and make small puris.
- Make a paste of 3 tbsps ghee and 3 tbsps plain flour. Apply this on all the puris and make a pile. Do the same with the other 3 parts.
- Take each pile and roll out into a large chapatti and cut into the following manner (as photo) so it will be 4 square pieces with the surround left over roll into small puris. Take a square and place one ball in the middle, then close the khaja bringing each corner into the middle.
- Make all the khaja in this manner.
- Heat oil or ghee and when ready fry khajas and with the help of a slotted spoon or knife, try to open from the top slightly so that it looks like a flower. Pour hot oil/ghee over it so the khaja have fried properly. When all have been fried and cooled, make a sugar syrup and then pour over the khajas and serve.

Anjeer (Fig) Cutlets

Ingredients:

500g milk powder
2 pkts anjeer (figs)
1 cup blanched almonds sliced
½ cup khaskhas (poppy seeds)
½ cup milk
3 plastic sheets
little green colouring
little yellow colouring
250g sugar
½ tsp nutmeg and cardamom

Method:

- Make sugar syrup with one bowl water – 1½ thread consistency. *(*for thread consistency - refer to page 71)*
- Divide syrup into two. To one part add green colour and yellow to the another. Mix 1 tbsp ghee and ½ cup milk to the milk powder.
- Add nutmeg and cardamom powder and divide this milk powder into three parts.
- In the first part of the milk powder add almonds and yellow colour syrup.
- Form a roll and lay on a plastic sheet.
- Now warm the green coloured syrup and the add second part of the milk powder then spread on the plastic sheet.
- Lay the yellow roll on the green mixture.
- Form a tight roll with the help of the plastic. Now chop the anjeer in a blender.
- In a saucepan put 2 tbsp ghee with the anjeer and roast till it is soft, then layer it on the plastic. Cover with another plastic sheet and roll it more thickly.
- Put the green colour roll on the anjeer and roll it again tightly.
- Once the roll is ready, sprinkle poppy seeds over the roll.
- After 4 hours, cut into ½" circle and your anjeer cutlets are ready.

Cattasa Roll

Ingredients:

500g milk powder
350g cashew nuts finely powdered
1 small tin cherries (cut into small rounds)
2 bowls sugar
one big plastic sheet
1 tbsp ghee
½ cup ghee
pinch of green colouring and pinch yellow colouring
¼ tsp nutmeg and cardamom powder

Method:

- In a pan make a sugar syrup with 1½ bowl water of 1½ thread consistency.
- Divide this syrup into three parts.
- Keep colourless syrup little more.
- Add yellow and green colouring to the other two parts of the sugar syrup.
- Take ½ bowl milk powder and add a little ghee and milk and mix well.
- Add nutmeg and cardamom.
- Take a little yellow syrup and add milk powder to it. Put this mixture in the middle of the plastic sheet and spread lengthwise. Arrange cherries on this.
- Make a thin roll with the help of the plastic sheet. Remove the plastic.
- In another pan take 1½ bowls milk powder.
- To this add the remaining ghee and milk. Add nutmeg and cardamom to the milk powder.
- Warm the green coloured syrup and add to the above milk powder.
- Put this on another plastic sheet and spread lengthwise.
- Now put the yellow roll onto this green colour and make a tight roll.
- In another pan put the cashew nut powder and the remaining milk powder with the nutmeg and cardamom powder.
- Add white syrup to this and follow the above procedure. Spread long on the plastic sheet.
- Put the green roll in the middle of the white roll and roll together.
- After 4 hours cut into equal parts.

Baklava

Ingredients:

1 pkt greek vermicelli-kataifi
1 bowl whole pistachios
greaseproof paper
1 baking tray
¼ bowl sugar
Little saffron
nutmeg and cardamom
2 tbsp honey
juice of 1 orange

Method:

- Form small baskets from the greek vermicelli.
- Soak the pistachios in the syrup and fill the basket with it.
- You will need 5 to 6 pistachios.
- Place on a baking tray and bake in the oven for 15mins at gas mark 5 until golden brown.
- Make a syrup of honey and orange juice and brush the baklava with it.

Masaledar Paak (Katlu)

Ingredients:

1 bowl wheat flour
1 bowl gram flour
1 bowl magaztari na bee
1 bowl coarsely ground
almonds
1 bowl coarsely ground
pistachios
1 ¼ bowls fried gum
arabic (gund)
1 bowl katlu
2 tbsp turmeric powder
4 tbsp ginger powder
mace
saffron

2 tbsp fenugreek powder
2 tbsp dillseed powder
2 tbsp fennel seed
powder
1 tsp black pepper
powder
2 bowls jaggery
ghee as required
nutmeg, cardamom
powder
1 bowl desiccated
coarsely ground coconut

Method:

- Roast both the flours in ghee until golden brown and add gum arabic a little at a time.
- Add desiccated coconut and almond mix and remove from the heat. Then add turmeric followed by the rest of the above ingredients, apart from the jaggery.
- In another pan heat the ghee and add the jaggery and switch off the gas. Add this to the above mixture and mix thoroughly.
- Line a tray with cellophane paper and then spread the mixture evenly and press with your hand on a steel bowl.
- Sprinkle poppy seeds, almonds and pistachio slices and once again press.
- When cool, cut into pieces and store in a container.

Pista Sandwich

Ingredients:

1 pkt greek vermicelli-kataifi
1½ bowl pistachios chopped
2 bowls sugar
20 cake cases
greaseproof paper
¼ tsp nutmeg, cardamom
few strands of saffron
baking tray

Method:

- Open the vermicelli gently and cut into 3" square pieces.
- Make sugar syrup.
- Add nutmeg, cardamom and saffron to the chopped pistachio.
- Now add just enough syrup to the pistachio to form a paste.
- Line the baking tray with greaseproof paper.
- Dip each piece of katalfi in the sugar syrup and lay on the baking tray.
- Spread pistachios on top of it.
- Cover with another piece of katalfi soaked in the syrup.
- Make all the sandwiches and bake in the oven at gas mark 4 to 5 for 20 minutes.
- Leave to cool and place in the cake cases.

Churma Na Ladoo

Ingredients:

1lb wheat flour
1 cup semolina
½ cup gram flour
1lb jaggery
1 ½ lb ghee
1 cup oil
2 tbsp poppy seeds
¼ tsp nutmeg and
cardamom

Method:

- Form a hard dough by mixing all three flours, with one cup of oil and warm water.
- Take a small portion and form oval shapes in the palm of your hands (muthia).
- Fry these in the ghee at a low temperature.
- Break these muthia and when they are cool, grind into a coarse mixture.
- Heat the ghee; when melted remove from the heat.
- Add the jaggery to the ghee.
- Mix the cardamom, nutmeg, jaggery and ghee to the muthia mixture.
- Make the mixture into round balls.
- Sprinkle poppy seeds on it.

Chand Ghari

Ingredients:

1 bowl milk powder
1 cup milk
1 tsp ground nutmeg
1 bowl ground sugar
thin slices of almonds and pistachios
1 bowl almonds coarsely ground
1 bowl pistachios coarsely ground
few strands of saffron
1 lb plain flour
2 tbsp ghee
ghee for frying
milk
2 tbsp sugar

Method:

• Mix the milk powder with 2 tbsp ghee and knead using the milk.
• Refrigerate for 3 hours.
• After 3 hours take out and grate.
• Mix almonds, pistachios and the grated milk powder and cook till it becomes pink in colour.
• Remove from the heat and add sugar, nutmeg, cardamom and saffron.
• Form walnut size balls.
• Add ghee to the plain flour.
• With the warm milk form a soft dough and divide into walnut sized balls.
• Take one portion and flatten in the palm of your hand.
• Put the ball in the middle and cover from all the sides using the dough.
• Make a small dent in the middle.
• Fry all ghari in the ghee at a low temperature.
• Take 3 tbsp ghee and mix with ground sugar.
• Dip each ghari in it.
• Take out and decorate with almond and pistachios or rose petals.

Anjeeram

Ingredients:

250gm almonds, coarsely ground & roasted
125gm pistachios coarsely ground & roasted
65gm cashew nuts, coarsely ground & roasted
250gm figs
190gm milk powder
65gm sugar
1½ cups milk
½ tsp nutmeg powder
2 tbsp ghee
½ tsp cardamon powder
saffron and green colouring

Method:

- Add 2 tbsp of ghee to the milk powder, mix thoroughly and knead into a ball.
- Refrigerate this for half hour, then remove and grate it.
- In a saucepan add some ghee and roast the grated mawa till light pink in colour.
- Meanwhile chop figs in a food processor.
- In a saucepan boil the milk and add the chopped figs and let it boil till the mixture thickens.
- Add sugar and let it boil a little while, then add it to the mawa and mix thoroughly.
- Now add all the nuts and rest of the above ingredients. Mix well and form balls to give shape to the anjeeram with the help of a mould.

Chamcham

Ingredients:

8 pints milk
Juice of 1 lemon or 1
tbsp citric acid
2 bowls sugar
yellow food colouring

Method:

- Boil the milk and gradually add lemon juice while stirring continuously.
- Continue to stir till milk curdles.
- Keep aside to cool.
- Strain the milk through a muslin lined sieve.
- Squeeze all the whey out.
- Press the curd (paneer) under a heavy flat weight for an hour.
- Knead the paneer with the your palm of your hand.
- Now add a drop of yellow colouring and form chamcham about 2" long.
- Boil 4 bowls of water in a big pan and add 2 bowls of sugar.
- When the water starts to boil, put the chamcham into the syrup for at least 10 minutes.
- Turn once and keep boiling for another 10 minutes without covering the pan.
- Remove from the heat.
- Once cold it is ready to serve.
- You can put silver paper on chamcham.

Trirangi Halvo Cake

Ingredients:

2lb carrots
1 bowl sugar
2 tbsp ghee
1½ cups milk powder
nutmeg, saffron and
cardamom powder
Small cup of double
cream
2 tbsp cocoa powder
blanched almonds or
almond flakes

Ingredients for dudhi:

1lb dudhi
½ bowl sugar
2 tbsp ghee
¾ cup milk powder
cardamom and pinch of
green colouring
2 tbsp double cream

Method:

• Grate carrots and roast with ghee, once cooked add double
  cream.
• Once the cream has been absorbed, add sugar.
• Keep cooking for 10 minutes, stirring continuously.
• Now add cardamom, saffron and nutmeg powder.
• Add milk powder and mix well. Follow the same method for
  dudhi. (page 129)
• Divide carrot halva into two parts. In one part add cocoa
  powder.
• Now arrange all three halva separately in the same size
  sandwich cake mould, lined with plastic paper. Once set, arrange
  in the serving dish: First put carrot halva in the dish; Layer with
  green halva turning upside down on the carrot halwa. Remove
  the plastic sheet; Now layer the third chocolate halwa on top
  of the green halwa using the same method. Decorate with the
  almond flakes.

Mohanthal with Khoya (Mawa)

Ingredients

500g gram flour
¼ lb khoya-mawa (milk powder)
250g sugar
½ cup ghee
250g ghee for roasting
½ cup milk
2 pinches yellow food colouring
½ tsp nutmeg and cardamom
¼ tsp mace powder (javitri)
almond and pistachio slices

Method:

- Heat ghee and milk in a pan and add to the gram flour.
- Mix well; press and keep aside for 20 minutes.
- Sieve mixture to make granules.
- Prepare sugar syrup on a low temperature with one cup of water of 2½ thread consistency. *(*for thread consistency - refer to page 71)*
- Add yellow colouring to the syrup.
- Roast flour with ghee until brown.
- Remove from the heat and add khoya and stir well.
- Mix syrup into the roasted flour.
- Mix well and slowly. Keep aside to cool down.
- Now add cardamom, mace, nutmeg and saffron.
- Keep butter paper in the tray and spread mohanthal.
- Decorate with almond and pistachio slices.
- Cut into pieces.

Karansai Ladoo

Ingredients:

1 cup coarse urad flour
½ cup coarse almond powder
½ cup coarse pistachio powder
¼ tsp cardamom powder
2 cups sugar
few strands of saffron
1 cup milk
2 cups ghee for frying
½ cup extra melted ghee

Method:

- Mix the urad flour and milk to form a thick batter.
- With the help of a Jara (a shallow spoon with holes for frying), fry bundi in the ghee.
- Once all the bundies are ready, crush in the food processor for few a seconds.
- Make a sugar syrup with one cup of water of 2 thread consistency.
  *(*for thread consistency - refer to page 71)*
- Now divide syrup into 2 parts.
- Soak bundi in one part of the syrup and add nuts in the other.
- Now mix all together.
- Add nutmeg, cardamom melted ghee and saffron to the bundi.
- Once warm roll into ladoos the size of walnuts.

Hira Sari

Ingredients:

250gm gram flour
250gm milk powder
250gm cashew nuts, coarsely ground
250gm almonds, coarsely ground
250gm pistachio, coarsely ground
125gm gum Arabic
375gm ground sugar
1tbsp ghee
½ cup milk
2 cups ghee
few strands of saffron
½ tsp cardamom and nutmeg
¼ tsp mace

Method:

- Add 1tbsp ghee and half a cup of milk to the milk powder for dhrabo.
- After 15-20 mins sieve this milk powder and keep aside.
- In a heavy based pan add ghee and gram flour and roast till it is golden brown.
- Then add arabic gum, a little at a time and then followed by the cashew nuts, almonds and pistachios.
- Roast for a while then add the milk powder and mix well.
- Remove from the heat and add all the spices.
- When it is almost cooled, add the sugar and start making small balls.
- Then put them in a mould to give shape.
- Decorate with silver balls.

Lalit Paak

Ingredients:

1 bowl plain flour
1 bowl wheat flour
1 bowl semolina
1 cup milk powder
1 bowl almond powder
1 bowl pistachio powder
1/4 tsp cardamom, few strands saffron
slices of almond and pistachio
1 bowl coarse urad dal flour
1 bowl coarse moong dal flour
1 bowl coarse gram dal flour
1/2 bowl dessicated coconut
1/2 bowl oil
3 bowls ghee

Perparation:

• Warm 2 tbsp ghee with 4 tbsp milk.
• Add this to the urad, gram and mung flour.
• Mix well and then sieve.
• Heat 1 bowl of ghee and add the above mixture. Cook until golden brown.
• Once cooked add the coconut, almond and pistachio powder and mix well.
• Remove from the heat.
• Mix oil with the wheat flour and semolina.
• Add warm water and form a firm dough.
• Form oval shapes with the dough.
• Deep fry until cooked. Cool and blend in a food processor to form a coarse power.
• Add 2 tbsp ghee to the milk powder.
• Mix well and add this to the roasted flours.
• Make a sugar syrup of 2 thread consistency and add this to all the mixture.
  (*for thread consistency - refer to page 71)
• Add a little ghee, cardamom, saffron, almond and pistachio slices and mix well.
• Spread on the butter paper tray and once cool, cut into desired pieces.

Curley Wurley Kaju Rolls (cashew nut rolls)

Ingredients:

3 bowls fine cashew nut powder
1 bowl sugar
2 drops of rose water
½ tsp pink colouring
pinch of nutmeg

Method:

- Make sugar syrup with ½ a cup water and 1 bowl of sugar.
- Divide this syrup into two parts.
- In one part add pink colour.
- In another part add half the cashew nut powder and nutmeg.
- Mix well to form a dough.
- Now lay a plastic sheet on a board and roll as thin as possible.
- Warm the pink syrup and add two drops of rose water.
- Now add the remaining cashew nut powder to the syrup and mix well.
- Lay another plastic sheet on the board and roll the pink dough as thin as possible.
- Now lift the pink sheet board and put it on top of the white one.
- Remove the plastic sheet from the top.
- Now start rolling tightly removing the plastic sheet as you roll.
- Once rolled cover the roll again with the plastic sheet to smoothen.
- Leave to set for 3 hours.
- Now slice in ½" rounds from the roll.

Shri-Khand

Ingredients:

8 pints milk
1 ½ bowls sugar
1 tsp cardamom powder
thin slices of almonds and pistachios
4 tbsp curd (yogurt)
¼ tsp nutmeg
few strands of saffron
1 pomegranate (optional)

Method:

- Bring the milk to the boil and keep aside to cool at room temperature.
- Add 4 tbsp of yogurt and mix very well; leave overnight.
- Spread the yogurt on a muslin cloth which has been placed on several layers of newspaper. The paper will soak any excess fluid. Leave for 2 hours.
- When the curd turns solid, sieve it through a fine sieve and add the sugar.
- Mix well.
- Put shrikhand in the bowl and add cardamom, saffron, and nutmeg.
- Sprinkle almonds and pistachios slices.
- If you like, add pomegranate seeds.
- You may add any fruit cut into small pieces.
- Chill in the fridge before serving.

Nutty Cones

Ingredients:

½ lb plain flour (1 tbsp ghee)
½ cup almonds
½ cup pistachios
½ cup cashew nuts
few raisins, walnut pieces,
glazed cherries
½ lb mawa or milk powder
1 cup ghee & few strands of saffron
½ cup desiccated coconut
2 cups sugar syrup
1 cup ground sugar
¼ tsp cardamom & nutmeg powder
¼ tsp rose essence
almond and pistachio slices

Method:

- Place the nuts in a food processor to form a coarse powder.
- In a pan roast mawa and, once it is pink in colour, add saffron, nutmeg, cardamom, raisins and ground sugar.
- Add ghee to the flour and form a firm dough with some water.
- Divide the dough in 4 equal parts and roll a very thin chapatti. Divide further into 4 pieces.
- Make a cone from each part.
- Now stuff the above mixture in the cone and seal the cone using a flour and water paste.
- Now deep fry in the ghee.
- Make a sugar syrup of one thread consistency and dip each cone in the syrup.
- Arrange in the tray and decorate with almond and pistachio slices.

Magaz Churmu

Ingredients:

Magaz:
500g gram flour
½ a cup milk
1 tbsp ghee
¼ tsp yellow colouring
1 tsp nutmeg powder
½ tsp mace and saffron
slices of almond and
pistachio

Churma:
500g wheat flour
½ cup semolina
½ cup oil
500gm sugar
2 cups of ghee
1 tsp cardamom
1 cup milk
ghee for frying

Method:

- Boil ½ cup milk and 1 tbsp ghee.
- Add this to the gram flour. Mix till it resembles breadcrumbs.
- Sieve the above mixture and roast with 2 cups of ghee till golden brown and then remove from the heat.
- Now mix semolina and wheat flour with ½ cup oil and knead into a hard dough with warm milk.
- Make rough balls and deep fry at a low temperature till golden brown and grind into a coarse powder.
- Mix the above roasted gram flour with this flour.
- Make a sugar syrup of 2 thread consistency with 2 cups water.
- Add the flours to the syrup and mix well.
- Add nutmeg, cardamom, saffron and mace powder.
- Spread in the plastic sheet lined tray.
- Smooth with a steel bowl and decorate with almond and pistachio slices.

Punch Tatwa Halvo

Ingredients:

4 pints of milk
½ tsp citric acid
1 bowl sugar
1 cup almond coarse powder
1 cup pistachio coarse powder
1 cup cashew nut coarse powder
1 tbsp ghee
½ cup raisins
2 tbsp charodi
¼ tsp cardamom and nutmeg powder
few strands of saffron

Method:

- In a pan boil the milk and as soon as it starts to boil, add citric acid to curdle it.
- Now strain paneer and rinse in the cold water.
- Place in a tea towel and remove excess fluid.
- Add ghee to the roasting pan and roast paneer at a low temperature till pink in colour.
- Now add all the nuts and raisins.
- Mix well and remove from the heat.
- Make a sugar syrup of 2 thread consistency and add to the above mixture. *(*for thread consistency - refer to page 71)*
- Now add cardamom, saffron and nutmeg and mix well.

Crystal Nuts Chikki

Ingredients:

1¼ bowl roasted peanuts
1 cup cashew nuts and
pistachios cut in half
1 bowl sugar
few strands of saffron
2 tbsp water

Method:

• Caramelise sugar with 2 tbsp water.
• Add the nuts.
• Spread the mixture on a greased wooden board and roll with a rolling pin.
• Cut into square pieces.

Penda and Microwave Penda (Brown)

Ingredients for Kesar Penda:

1lb milk powder
1 pint milk
250g sugar
1 teaspoon cardamom powder
few strands of saffron
1 tbsp ghee
1 small cup single cream
almond and pistacho for decoration

Ingredients (brown Penda)
500ml fresh double cream
1 cup milk powder
½ cup sugar
saffron, cardamom
(use the same cup of double cream
for the measurement)

Method for Kesar Penda:

• Make medium sugar syrup with milk.
• Add saffron to the syrup.
• Mix ghee and cream with the milk powder. Then add cardamom powder.
• When the syrup is reduced to 1½ cups, add to the milk powder.
• Form small penda and decorate with almond and pistacho.

Method for brown Penda:
• Mix cream and sugar and bring just to the boiling point.
• Remove from the heat.
• Now add the milk powder and cream mixture in a big glass bowl.
• Place in the microwave for 2 mins.
• Gently stir with spoon twice and again put in the microwave for another 2 mins.
• Repeat this a further 6 times so that it has had a total of 16mins cooking time.
• Once done, add saffron and cardamom powder and mix well.
• If the mixture is not thick enough to roll penda, add little milk powder.
• This penda will be brown in colour.

Chocolate-Coated Katli

Ingredients:

1 lb cashew nut powder
1 pkt cooking chocolate
1 ½ bowl sugar
1 bowl water
¼ tsp nutmeg

Method:

- Make a sugar syrup of two thread consistency.
  (*for thread consistency - refer to page 71)
- Mix with cashew nut powder and nutmeg.
- Make dough.
- Spread butter paper in a tray.
- Spread mixture till smooth.
- Melt chocolate on a steamer and spread on the cashew nut mixture.
- Cut into a diamond shape.

Motiya Ladoo (orange colour)

Ingredients:

1 lb gram flour
1 bowl almonds, in slices
1 bowl pistachio, thin slices
1 bowl sugar
½ cup of oil
¼ tsp cardamom and nutmeg
¼ tsp yellow food colouring
2 tbsp raisins
few strands of saffron

Method:

- Sift gram flour and mix with half a cup of oil.
- With warm water, form a stiff dough.
- Make fist shape balls with a finger depression and deep fry.
- When cool, place in a food processor to form a coarse powder.
- Sieve the powder.
- Make two thread consistency sugar syrup and add yellow food colouring.
- Add syrup to the powder and mix with three tablespoons of melted ghee.
- Add almonds, pistachio and all the above ingredients.
- Mix thoroughly.
- Make small ladoos while the mixture is still warm.

Finger Rolls

Ingredients:

1 bowl coarsly ground almonds
1 bowl coarsly ground pistachios
1 bowl coarsly ground cashew nuts
1 bowl ground sugar
1 pkt filo pastry
2 tbsp butter
3 tbsp golden syrup

Method:

- Mix all nuts with sugar.
- Separate filo pastry.
- Brush butter on the sheet of the filo pastry.
- Spread mixed powder on the pastry and roll until it is the width of a finger.
- Cut 3" rolls and brush with the butter.
- Put all the rolls on the buttered paper tray.
- Bake in the oven at gas mark 5 for 20 minutes till pink in colour.
- Brush with sugar syrup made with orange juice or use golden syrup.

Mathadi

Ingredients:

1 bowl whole wheat flour
½ bowl sesame seeds crushed
ghee for frying and to add to the flour
rose petals for decoration
1 bowl sugar for syrup
2 pinches cardamom
few strands of saffron
a few pistachios and almonds
¼ cup warm water

Method:

- In a large pan mix flour and crushed sesame seeds.
- Add enough ghee so that flour looks like breadcrumbs and with water, knead to form a hard dough.
- Now roll a very big chapatti and spread ghee on it.
- Make a roll and cut the small rounds with a knife.
- Roll each round slightly.
- Now deep fry in the ghee until golden brown.
- Make a sugar syrup of 3 thread consistency and dip the mathdi in the syrup. *(*for thread consistency - refer to page 71)*
- Lay a plastic sheet in the tray and arrange all the mathdies on it.
- Decorate with rose petals, almonds and pistachios slices.

Khajali unsalted

Ingredients:

3 bowls plain flour
1 ½ bowl ghee
oil for frying
1 bowl warm water
another ½ a bowl water

Method:

- In a pan take 2 bowls of plain flour and add one bowl of ghee.
- Mix well.
- Knead dough with one bowl of cold water.
- In another pan take the remaining flour.
- Add ½ bowl of ghee and ½ bowl of cold water and mix well.
- Heat the mixture for few a minutes till the ghee separates.
- Remove from the heat & leave to cool.
- Now flatten the dough on the worktop and sprinkle the baked flour over it.
- Gather all the sides and again flatten the dough.
- Again sprinkle the baked flour and gather all the sides.
- Repeat the process several times till all the baked dough is used.
- Cover the dough and keep a side for ½ an hour.
- Take a small round lump from the dough and press it with three fingers to make holes.
- Heat oil in a broad frying pan and fry all the khajali at a very low temperature.
- Keep all the fried khajali upright so that all the excess oil drips down for 4 hours.

Dudhi Halvo (Gourd)

Ingredients:

1lb dudhi (gourd)
½ bowl sugar
1-2 tbsp butter
2 bowls milk
2 pinches cardamom
few strands of saffron
1 pinch of green colouring
slices of almond and pistachio
2 tbsp milk powder

Method:

- Grate dudhi and add milk, ghee and green colouring and boil mixture. Stir continuoulsy.
- Once the milk evaporates, add sugar and keep cooking.
- When thick enough add milk powder, saffron and cardamom.
- Now place in a bowl and decorate with slices of almonds and pistachios.

Kala Kand

Ingredients:

4 pints of milk
1 small cup double cream
1 bowl sugar
½ cup icing sugar
½ tsp citric acid
1 tsp rose essence
paper cups for cake
1 tbsp pistachio slices
1 small plastic sheet
a pinch of nutmeg

Method:

- In a pan heat milk and once it comes to boiling point add citric acid to curdle.
- Now strain all the water from the paneer and wash with cold water.
- Put the paneer on the cloth and dry completely.
- Paneer should be completely dry and crumbled.
- In another pan make 2 thread consistency of sugar syrup.
  *(*for thread consistency - refer to page 71)*
- Add paneer to the syrup and leave for three minutes.
- Then strain paneer and leave to cool completely.
- Ensure the syrup has been drained.
- Mix double cream, icing sugar and rose essence and nutmeg and whisk until it has thickened.
- Add paneer to this mixture and mix well.
- Lay plastic sheet in the tray and spread kala kand.
- Decorate with pistachios and leave the tray in the fridge.
- Once cool and set, cut into squares and put in the paper cups.

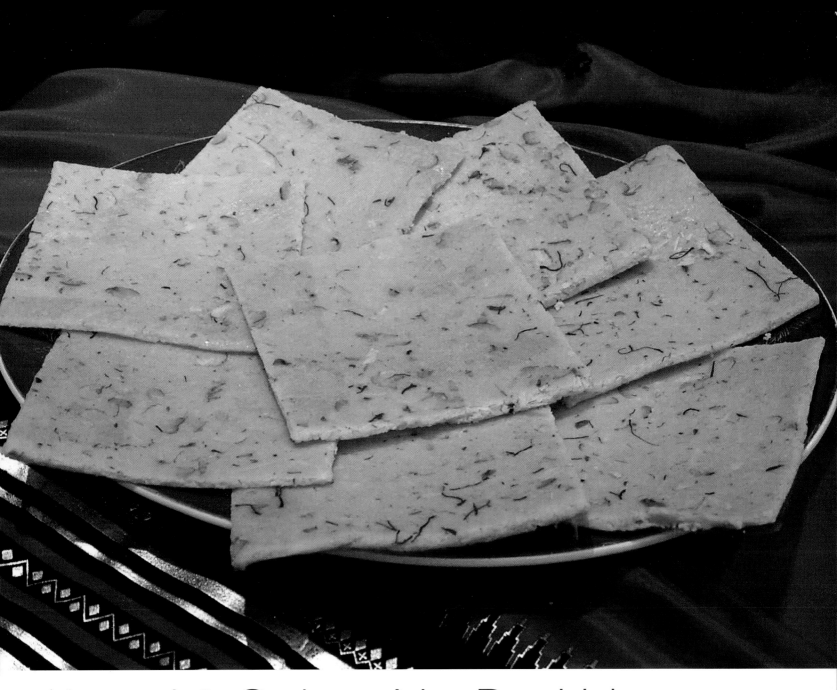

Almond & Cashew Nut Dry Halvo

Ingredients:

2 bowls almond powder
2 bowls cashew powder
1 bowl sugar
2 pints of milk
few strands of saffron
½ tsp cardamom powder
few almond and pistachio slices

Method:

• Soak almonds in hot water and remove skin.
• Now place cashew nuts and almonds in a food processor to form a fine powder.
• Add ghee and cardamom powder and mix well.
• In a pan, boil milk and sugar till it becomes quite thick.
• Now mix the nut powder well and remove from the heat.
• On the work top, lay plastic sheet and put the mixture on it.
• Apply ghee and roll thin.
• Add slices of almond and pistachio, cover with plastic and roll again so that slices are pressed evenly.
• Once cool cut into squares.

Rang Tarang

Ingredients:

2 bowls of very fine vermicelli
1 bowl gram flour
1 bowl milk powder
1 bowl coarsely ground almonds
1 bowl pistachios coarse
1 bowl of desicated coconut
2 bowls of ground sugar
few strands of saffron
1/4 tsp cardamom and nutmeg
2 pinches of mace
1 bowl ghee

Method:

• Knead milk powder with cold milk and keep refrigerated for 2 hours then grate.
• Roast gram flour until golden brown.
• Add almonds, pistachios and coconut.
• Mix well and remove from the heat.
• Add 2 tbsp ghee to grated mawa and roast for 5-10 minutes till ghee separates, and the colour becomes pink.
• Add this to the roasted gram flour.
• Add sugar, saffron, cardamom, mace and nutmeg.
• Cut into shapes or mould into small balls.

Sweet Satta

Ingredients:

3 bowls plain flour
1 ½ bowls ghee
1 ½ bowls water
oil for frying
1 lb sugar
thin slices of almond
and pistachio

Method:

- In a pan take 2 bowls of plain flour, then add one bowl of ghee and mix well.
- Knead dough with one bowl of cold water.
- In another pan take the remaining flour.
- Roast the second mixture for a few minutes till it turns brown and separate.
- Remove from the heat and let it cool down completely.
- Now flatten the dough on the worktop and sprinkle the baked flour over it.
- Gather all the sides and again flatten the dough.
- Sprinkle the baked flour and gather all the sides.
- Repeat the process several times till all the baked dough is used.
- Cover the dough and keep aside for ½ hour.
- Take a small round lump from the dough and press it with three fingers to make hole.
- Heat oil in the broad frying pan and fry all the satta at a very low temperature.
- Keep all fried sattas upright so that all the excess oil drips down; at least for 4 hours.
- Make a thick sugar syrup.
- Dip each satta into the syrup.
- Remove and decorate with almond and pistachio slices.
- You may decorate with rose petals.

Madarasi Paak

Ingredients:

1lb gram flour
1½ bowls sugar
1 bowl chopped almonds
½ pint milk
½ bowl chopped pistachios
1 bowl ghee
1 cup gum arabic (coarse powder)
1 tbsp ghee and ½ cup milk
few almonds
½ cup desiccated coconut
½ cup milk powder
few strands saffron

Method:

- Blanch almonds, remove the skin and finely slice.
- Boil half of the milk and ghee; once boiled remove and add to the gram flour for mixture (dhrabo).
- Mix well and put through a coarse sieve.
- In a big pan put ghee and roast the gram flour till pink.
- At this point add edible gum a little by little so that it is also roasted.
- In another pan make sugar syrup with sugar and milk.
- Once the syrup thickens, add almonds and pistachios.
- Boil for a little while till the syrup thickens.
- Add this to the gram flour.
- Mix well.
- Add milk powder, coconut and saffron.
- At this point the ghee will separate.
- Let the mixture cool down so that all the ghee merges into the flour.
- Now in the tray lay a plastic sheet and spread the madrasi Paak.
- Once cool cut into pieces.

Barfi Churmu

Ingredients:

3 bowls wheat flour
1 bowl gram flour
1 bowl plain flour
1 bowl semolina
2½ bowls sugar
ghee as required (1½ lb ghee)
1½ cups oil
½ cup ghee
½ tsp nutmeg and cardamom
almond and pistachio slices

Method:

- Mix all flours in a bowl.
- Add oil and make into a soft dough using warm water.
- Knead well adding a little ghee.
- Divide the dough into equal balls and form muthia.
- Fry on a low temperature till brown.
- Break and leave to cool.
- Put the balls in a food processor and blend to form a coarse powder.
- Make sugar syrup of 2½ thread consistency.
- Heat ghee and add to the mixture as required.
- Now add nutmeg and cardamom.
- Add the syrup to the flour mixture.
- Spread on a tray and garnish with almonds and pistachios.

Raffaelo Chocolate

Ingredients:

petit four sweet cases
1 cup roasted walnuts/almonds
200g white cooking chocolate
3 cups desiccated coconut
1 bowl sweetened condensed milk
1 bowl flaked almonds

Method:

- Mix condensed milk and coconut to make a soft dough.
- Roast walnuts in a little butter.
- Make small balls and place a walnut in the centre.
- Cover completely with the dough.
- Melt the chocolate in a bowl over simmering water.
- Cover each ball with chocolate and dip in the flaked almonds.
- Place in a petit four case.

Kesar Mani

Ingredients:

2 cups ground almonds (without skins)
¾ cup ground cashew nuts
1 cup fried gum arabic
1 cup gram flour
1 cup milk power
½ cup fine vermicelli (leave 1 tbsp for garnish)
1½ cups of ghee
1½ cups icing sugar
1 cup fresh coconut grated and then oven roasted
2½ tsps ground cinnamon
few strands saffron

2 pinches ground cardamom
1 tbsp flaked almonds and pistachios

Method:

- Boil the milk with 2 tbsp ghee; add to the gram flour and milk powder and stir well.
- In a large pan, add 4 tbsp ghee and add the above mixture.
- Cook gently until the mixture turns light pink.
- Add a little more ghee if required.
- Add ground almonds and cashew nuts, remove from the heat.
- Add fried gum arabic, icing sugar, saffron, cardamom, coconut, cinnamon and vermicelli and stir well.
- Put mixture into and plastic lined baking tray and leave to set.
- Garnish with flaked almonds, pistachios and vermicelli.
- Cut into squares.

Kesar Kali (Almond Plait)

Ingredients:

250g butter
250g packet dairy milk chocolate
1 cup of dates stoned
1 cup almonds coarsely chopped
1 cup pistachios coarsely chopped
1 cup cashew nuts coarsely chopped
2½ cups of rice crisps
few strands of saffron
¼ tsp cardamom
1 cup desiccated coconut

Method:

• Heat the butter on a low temperature until melted.
• Add dates, stir continually until they become soft.
• Add chocolate until its melted, then add all the nuts, the rest of the ingredients and mix in well.
• Remove from the heat.
• Make small round flattened balls and roll in desiccated coconut.
• Place on a lined baking tray and leave to set.

Khajurmamra Ni Puri

Ingredients:

1 bowl self rasing flour
1 bowl ground almonds
(without skins)
1 tsp butter
½ tsp ground nutmeg
½ tsp vanilla essence
large pinch saffron
mixed with 2 tbsp of milk
sugar syrup (¾ bowl sugar mixed
with ½ bowl water)
sunflower oil for frying

Method:

• Mix all the ingredients except the sugar syrup and ground pistachios.
• Add water to make a soft dough.
• Roll out the dough to ½ cm thickness in a square shape.
• Cut ½ inch strips and plait 3 strips together.
• Deep fry the plaits, cool and dip in the sugar syrup.
• Garnish with the ground pistachios.

Crunchy Barfi

Ingredients:

8 weetabix
1 can of condensed sweetened milk
1 cup desiccated coconut
125g melted butter
125g rich tea biscuits
2 cups mixed almonds, pistachios
and cashew nuts (coarsely ground)
2 tsp ghee
pinch each of nutmeg, cardamom
and saffron

Method:

• Warm milk, butter and ghee until it boils.
• Turn off the heat and add the rest of the ingredients.
• Put the mixture in a plastic lined baking tray and leave to set.
• Cut into squares.

Patisa

Ingredients:

250gms gram flour
375gms sugar (enough water to cover sugar)
1 ½ lb ghee
½ lb almonds – cut into two
¼ lb pistachios – cut into two
few strands of saffron
pinch of yellow food colouring
4 pinches of nutmeg and cardamom powder

Method:

- In a heavy pan make sugar syrup till three thread consistency.
- Add food colour, saffron, cardamom and nutmeg powder.
- In another pan roast gram flour with ghee till light brown.
- In another pan warm one cup of ghee.
- Once the flour is roasted add sugar syrup and hot ghee.
- Spread the mixture thinly in a tray.
- Decorate with almonds and pistachios.
- Cut into pieces.
- When cool, store in an airtight container.

Peanut Paak

Ingredients:

1lb (jugu) peanuts
1 bowl sugar
¼ tsp nutmeg

Method:

- Roast peanuts in the microwave and remove all the husks.
- Grind in the grinder to form a coarse powder.
- In a saucepan make a sugar syrup of 1½ thread consistency.
  (*for thread consistency - refer to page 71)
- Mix nutmeg powder with the peanut powder.
- Now add the peanut powder to the syrup.
- Mix well and spread in the butter paper lined tray.
- Once cold cut into pieces.

Phool Bahar

Ingredients:

I bowl cashew nuts finely ground
¾ bowl sugar
¼ bowl water
I pinch nutmeg powder

Ingredients for pistachio masala:

¼ cup pistachios coarsely ground
I pinch cardamom powder
½ pinch yellow and green colouring
I tbsp oil

Method:

- Mix sugar and water in a saucepan and put on a slow heat to make a syrup of I ½ thread consistency. When ready take 3 tbsp of the syrup in a small saucepan and add the yellow and green colouring. Mix, then add the ground pistachios with the oil and cardamom powder. Mix thoroughly and keep aside.
- In a basin put the cashew nut powder and add nutmeg powder, then gradually add the sugar syrup and form a similar dough.
- If the sugar syrup remains, keep it a side and use if necessary.
- Take a mould in whichever shape you want. Put the mould in a plastic bag and hold the bag all round. Put the cashew nut dough in the mould and press with three fingers. Make a hole in the middle with a rolling pin and put the pistachio masala in the middle.
- Press properly and then arrange them on plastic paper.
- Consume after half ans hour.

Index

Index